PRAISE FOR KATHY FARROKHZAD AND
HORSE LISTENING: THE BOOK

"Sometimes it is nothing short of spooky how [Kathy] puts into written words the concepts that I am trying to explain. Her ability to answer the exact questions that my students are asking is amazing! All of the basics plus some fresh new twists are covered and presented in a clear, concise and entertaining fashion.

I highly recommend this book for anyone who is learning, teaching or simply enjoying his or her journey with horses. It is full of practical suggestions and ideas that apply to all equestrian disciplines and to all riders whether they are at the very beginning of their relationship with horses or, as in my case, have spent a lifetime learning, improving and passing on their understanding of this wonderful creature we call 'the horse'." - Cathy Drumm, Equestrian Instructor, Trainer and Clinician

"What I love about Kathy's writing is her honesty. She writes about what she knows – her experiences with riding and training for years and years in search of the seamless equine partnership. (Aren't we all?) Now add Kathy's talent for putting a sentence together, and we are virtually sharing her journey. There is such a feeling of presence in her writing!

As many books as I have read on the subject of riding, none has been as clear as this one. It has a flow that really appeals. Eminently 'readable,' I find myself actually, yes! –reading it aloud!

I want it in audio form, so I can take it out to the arena and practice astride, step by step, line by line. In the meantime, however, I shall be very, very happy to sit and imagine myself in the saddle, resisting…flowing…resisting…flowing." - Jet Tucker, Rider and Horse Owner

Horse Listening: *The Book*

STEPPING FORWARD TO EFFECTIVE RIDING

KATHY FARROKHZAD

Photographs by Natalie Banaszak
Illustration by Jeff Thompson

A Collection of Articles From
Horse Listening: The Blog

Published by:
Full Circle Equestrian
P.O. Box 216
Ballinafad, ON, Canada N0B 1H0

www.horselistening.com

DEDICATION

For my parents, who are the foundation of
everything I am and can be.

Beauty

CONTENTS

Section 3: The Specifics   81

Section 4: The Solutions   106

Section 5: The Results   157

WITH THANKS

It's true that it takes a village to raise a child. It is also true that a village might be just what is required to produce a book!

Although I have written and formulated the words in this book, there are several people to whom I am indebted for their significant influence on the creation of this book.

To Eva Peter, who, over a course of 6 years, 4 times a week, embedded much of what I now "know" into my physical and mental being: thank you for your patience, hard work, explanations, challenges and passion for the horse. You developed my skills to a level that I never imagined I could reach and continue to support me in many ways beyond horseback. This book is largely the result of your work with me.

To Carol Campeau, whose friendship has always been a source of strength and inspiration for me: thank you for your wisdom, presence and persuasion that gently sent me on the path that became Horse Listening.

To Kaleigh Arbuckle, partner in (horsey) time, fellow lover of equines, coach, trainer, mentor and friend: thank you for your always positive, honest and selfless feedback.

To José Villeneuve, fellow horse lover, trainer and coach: thank you for your nudges, guidance and vision for me and the book.

To my parents, who believed in this book more than I did: thanks for your encouragement, celebrations, prodding, deadlines and feedback.

To Jet Tucker, who literally came out of cyberspace to support, edit and encourage my first project: thanks for being there in the right place at the right time.

To the readers of Horse Listening, who came in "herds" out of the virtual woodwork to read, comment and critique my articles: without your suggestions and encouragement, there would be no book.

To the horses (especially Kayla, Annahi, Roya and Cyrus): thank you for allowing me to grow and learn on the back of your equine wisdom.

SAFETY FIRST

In all of this book's chapters, as in all riding, concern for the horse's well-being, health and longevity is at the forefront of our efforts. It is also the method behind the madness of all the suggestions contained in this book.

As with all physical endeavors, horseback riding requires a certain level of fitness, balance and coordination. The unpredictable nature of the horse always adds an element of uncertainty and danger that we need to be aware of.

Please use any and all of the suggestions in this book at your discretion. Feel free to change anything to meet the needs of you and your horse. Finally, be sure to "listen", because the horse will always let you know if you are on the right track.

FORWARD

If you want to ride horses, you had better be prepared for much more than just learning the skills and steps that come with developing physical expertise. Because riding is not instant-gratification friendly, it is not the type of activity that is easily mastered. In fact, some people contend that the special call of horseback riding is that it can never be perfected.

Change horses, and be prepared to learn a whole new set of riding skills that you never needed on your previous horse. Change disciplines, and be content with starting to learn the basic skills all over again!

During my path as an equestrian, as I waded into the various disciplines that eventually led me to where I am now, I learned one truth that pervades through it all: there are many more commonalities between horses, riders and disciplines than there are differences.

We don't always recognize this truth. We bicker, critique and criticize, propagate stereotypes and think what we do is better than what "they" do.

Because the grass *is* greener on our side of the fence, no? I want to say, "No."

Good riding is good riding is good riding, as they say.

Despite our differences in disciplines, all good riders share many characteristics that contribute to their success. It really does not matter if they live in one part of the world or another. Language has nothing to do with it and neither does race.

The truth is that the horse is a great equalizer. He couldn't care less who you are, what baggage you bring to the table, and what you think you know. He does only one thing – he responds well to good care and treatment. Or he doesn't.

It was my quest to be a good horse keeper that led me to writing the Horse Listening blog. Although I am truly challenged by learning riding skills and techniques to the best of my ability, even now, over 20 years later and a culmination of days and days of clinics, lessons and stall muckings later, I do not believe that I am a "great" rider. I leave that for people who have dedicated their professional lives to riding and training – both themselves and their horses.

In contrast, I believe myself to be among the majority of "the rest of us." I work full time in a non-horsey profession, which allows me to have enough resources to be able to own horses but limits my time and energy. Time spent with them revolves around my other obligations, and my riding schedule often suffers.

I imagine there are many of us in this boat. We are passionate horse lovers who also want to develop ourselves into the best riders we can be, given our sometimes-limited resources. In our quest for reaching our highest potential in whatever horse-related avenue we pursue, we have at the root of our motivations the well being of the horse.

So with the belief that I have learned enough to have valid experiences and skills to share, and with the final urging of my good friend, Carol, who told me, "Just do it," I first started the blog and then began to collect the successful articles into the compilation that has turned into this book.

It is my hope that there is plenty in here for you to relate to, learn from and share with friends. Wishing you years of horse listening pleasure!

- *Kathy Farrokhzad*

INTRODUCTION

"I want to ride horses," she said, with a glint in her eyes and a sureness that came from an unknown place deep within.

It mattered not that she did not have a horse or any idea what it felt like to walk, trot and canter on a living, breathing animal ten times heavier than herself.

So she convinced her parents to buy the breeches, the boots and the helmet. She found a wonderful barn teeming with energetic and dedicated girls who had one common characteristic that drove their every action: the love for the horse.

It was horses she wanted to ride, and that was what she was going to do. Even before her first official lesson, she knew she was in the right place.

*****

Many of us began our riding careers in the same manner as that little girl. In fact, just like her, some of us might share the same fascination and love for the horse that drives us to challenge ourselves far beyond even our own expectations.

Although it takes years of patient and diligent practice, hours of sweat and kind guidance from giving instructors, the results are quite truly worth the work. Because once you've learned to coordinate all your body parts, you are well on your way to becoming the rider that all horses dream of - the one that makes them feel good and improves not only their physical abilities but also their very way of interacting with the world around them.

But there is more to riding than the horse's progress. It is difficult to express the depth of personal development I have experienced through my path in horses and riding. However, I expect that if you have spent time with horses, interacting with them, riding them, *living* with them, then you are probably quite familiar with the learning and self-improvement that is part and parcel of being a "horseback rider".

This book is derived from my ramblings on my Horse Listening blog. Inspired by my own riding, training and teaching experiences, I decided to put into words the ideas I have gleaned over the years from conversations and discussions with friends, instructors and riders - all fellow horse lovers with one underlying purpose: to be the best we can be for our horses.

Since the book is written from my experiences, you might notice that I am writing from the perspective of a dressage and previously western/natural horsemanship/endurance rider. Therefore, although most of my specific aid sequences and suggestions are derived from the basics of dressage, I believe that much of what I write here is relevant to all disciplines precisely because it is built on the fundamentals of riding. Although I am very aware that there are a multitude of paths to horse riding heaven, I hope many of these ideas are relevant to your discipline and your personal situation.

This book focuses specifically on riding as a means of improving the horse. The exercises and ideas in it are purposely hand-picked to help you develop your own path to becoming an effective rider, not only for the benefits you will glean personally, but also to enable you to make positive changes *through riding* that will enhance your horse's development as well.

If you don't have an instructor, these ideas can act as a starting point. Although it is always preferable to have "eyes on the ground," it is possible for you to try some of these lessons and self-evaluate as you go along. Listen to your horse, and you'll get the answers you need!

* * * *

There are many reasons why we enjoy riding horses. Maybe one of the most appealing facets of riding is the sense of freedom: freedom from our own limitations, freedom from gravity, freedom to (literally) roam the earth. Time stands still while we have the privilege of feeling movement from the back of our four-legged friend. Riding gives us the place to just be.

Of course, there are other purposes too. Some of us revel in the challenge of learning the skills required to becoming a good team member of this unlikely duo. Riding is like no other sport or recreational pursuit simply because of the equine partner that must not only carry us, but also do so effortlessly and gracefully. As we develop our specific skill sets, we also grow as human beings in character, emotional maturity and mental acuity.

But there is one other motivation that drives some of us to persevere in the never-ending learning process that is horseback riding: improving the horse. As your own skills develop, you begin to realize that not only can you meet your own needs through riding, but also that you can even become an instrument of benefit for the horse.

Through riding, it is possible to make physical changes to the horse that he might never achieve naturally. Not only will he become fitter and more athletic through the process, but he may develop a stronger top line, a fuller hind end and a more supple body. Old injuries fade to distant memory as his new physical prowess resolves problems literally one day at a time.

But there is more! Along with the physical changes comes mental and emotional development. Horses that are ridden well invariably become calmer, more confident, bolder and more relaxed in the way they live in their world.

Who doesn't want to be that instrument of change for their horse?

There is no replacement for actual riding lessons where the instructor is present and addressing your needs from a moment-to-moment basis.

However, in a typical riding lesson, there is little time to devote to the nitty-gritty details that go into each skill. Often, we are caught in the moment, trying to make the best use of our time with our instructor.

However, you may have unanswered questions after the lesson, and if you are not lucky enough to have daily access to your instructor, the problems might remain until your next lesson session. Sometimes, although you are taught the theory, there may be details that are not mentioned or overlooked.

This is where this book fits into your riding program. Each topic discussed in this book is designed to take you deeper into a fundamental aspect of riding. The aim of this book is to be that middle ground of knowledge that is required before you get on the horse's back. Sometimes, it might be useful as a guide to come back to after you ride, to serve as an opportunity for reflection and feedback.

The conundrum of riding is that everything is interconnected. The physical challenge is that there really is no aid that goes in isolation - every part of your body is working toward a combined goal, whether you know it or not. However, as a riding student, you may wish to focus on one or two aspects each day, and develop some mastery of those skills before moving on to other skills.

Therefore, the structure of this book is designed so that there is focus on one aspect per chapter. We examine that particular skill or aid in depth, sometimes to the exclusion of other skills (for the moment), so that we can do the thinking off the horse's back. Your reading time is your chance to analyze, plan and goal set.

Once you are on your horse's back, you need to act, evaluate, renew your efforts and sometimes change your natural reactions. The top of the horse is not the place to sit and deliberate on pros and cons. Instead, do your 'homework' here, while reading the book. Then head to the barn and put it together as you ride.

The book is divided into five sections. *Section I: The Reason* is an analysis of why we are so enamored by horses. What drives us to put in the time and effort needed to rise to the challenge of becoming the best rider we can be?

Section 2: The Essentials is devoted to some of the basic riding skills that form the way we communicate with the horse. These techniques are the building blocks of future success. Next, we look at *Section 3: The Specifics* - particular exercises that develop the quality of the horse's movement.

Section 4: The Solutions presents several chapters that give insight into correcting common problems. Try some of these exercises to develop good rhythm, hind end engagement and turns. A section on rein lameness analyzes something that is very common but rarely discussed. These solutions might help to put you on track toward developing your horse's highest potential.

Lastly, we pause to take a look back at *The Result* of our work: what have we learned through this process? What happens when we dedicate ourselves to a regular routine of self-improvement and development of the horse?

A special feature of this book is the *In The Ring* section at the conclusion of many chapters. This section is designed to give you suggestions on how you can take the ideas in the chapter into the riding ring. No book can ever take the place of a live teacher. However, what this book can do is give you action plans, comments and strategies that you can take with you to your rides.

Wishing you many happy rides and years of horse listening!

Section 1: The Reasons

1 The Pinnacle of Horseback Riding

Why do we ride horses?

There must be as many reasons to ride horses are there are people who ride. For those of us that are bitten with "the bug" that is horses, there are few reasons *not* to get on a horse's back!

Here are the top ten motivators that keep equestrians coming back for more. Do any of the following reasons resonate with you?

10. The chance to be in the great outdoors.

Spring, summer, winter or fall - you can find a myriad of activities to do with horses. As you participate in your various activities, you become so much more a part of the outdoor environment.

Spring is a time of temperatures rising and the softening of frost-covered ground. What was once a rock-hard snow-covered field becomes a mud-laden, slippery surface, which hints at impending grassy growth in coming weeks.

Summer is a time of warmth, ease and comfort, although in our parts, the insects run rampant so we have to protect the horses with fly sheets and masks. Summer is nevertheless a time of high activity and lots of horsing around.

Fall comes with bittersweet messages - on the one hand, nature is in her most beautiful glory with full foliage and the changing colors of leaves. On the other hand, longer and cooler nights signal a time of respite for the plants and thicker coats for our horses. However, some of our best riding takes place during autumn while the weather is still warm enough for good footing, but cool enough to encourage energetic horses and inspired riding.

The winter brings with it the first snowfall and a complete change of scenery. Winter riding through untouched fresh snow is an experience in itself. Bundled up and riding our furry winterized horses, we appreciate the beauty of Mother Nature in all her white washed glory.

Although conditions might not always be the best, you learn to work with the weather and appreciate natural artwork. You also learn to take better care of yourself as well as your horses in response to the weather conditions of the season.

9. The joy of being in the world of horses.

You learn new communication skills when you interact with horses. By their very nature, horses are not the same as the pets we are familiar with. They are large, they are prey animals and they allow us to ride them!

Spend a few days with horses and you'll easily begin to recognize their social signals. You'll be able to identify the lead horse. You will watch as "the greeter" horse keeps track of the herd and makes sure everyone is accounted for.

Soon enough, you will know how you can assume a role in the herd and communicate using horse language. You will discover a life of routine, social structure and being in the moment. What a nice change from our hectic day-to-day roller coaster work schedules!

There is nothing quite like the ultimate release – from both the horse and the rider!

8. The privilege of being allowed to sit on the back of such a magnificent animal and seeing the world from his perspective.

Life on four legs, several hands high is certainly different than what we are used to! Not only does the act of riding bring us new and (at first) unfamiliar experiences, but the places you can literally go is good enough reason to ride.

Thanks to horses and riding, I have traveled all over my own province, in other provinces, and in other countries.

From horse shows to riding clinics to week-long equine expos, there is never a lack of things to do, places to go and new friends to make! Certainly without horses as a reason to pursue these activities, our lives would be lacking.

7. Exercise that is so similar to our own movement that it is healing for ourselves.

Riding horses gives our body the movement it relishes and needs. In the case of hippotherapy, riding can literally be therapeutic.

Riding as a sport also benefits the body and the mind in many ways. The horse's movement, especially at the walk, is similar to the mechanics of our own bi-ped walk. For people who have difficulty walking, riding a horse can be a way to maintain physical coordination and suppleness especially in the hips and lower body.

At the most basic sense, we often talk about our horses being our therapists. There is quite a lot of truth to the mental and emotional development brought on through our interactions with horses - even to the extent of horses helping people with social skill problems and leadership development.

6. The variety of activities and events you can participate in if you ride a horse.

Once you get involved in the horse world, you will be amazed at all the activities and events that you might participate in! From weekly riding lessons to trail riding to vaulting to fundraising rides - the sky is the limit! There are simply too many events to list here. The clincher is that those who don't participate in riding do not have the opportunity to even begin to understand such vibrant experiences.

5. Learning skills that promote coordination, timing, rhythm, balance, core strength and much more.

Skills, skills and skills!

Skill development is one large component of what horseback riding is all about. As you grow as a rider, you'll be amazed at how your physical abilities progress. You will be sure to improve in all the above areas as well as in your mental skills such as problem-solving and determination.

4. The self-development process that goes hand-in-hand with skill development.

Self-confidence, self-control, patience, empathy - all these and more traits will be developed as you progress through your riding experiences. There is no way around it. If you ride, you will grow as a human being.

3. The life-long, ever-changing learning process that is horses and riding.

If you like learning, and feel a pang of excitement when you discover something new, horse riding is for you! The catch is that you would do well to enjoy the feeling of discomfort-before-learning-something-new (some people call it frustration) because it will happen again and again - even years into your riding career!

2. Learning to problem solve effectively and ride with enough tact to improve the health and well-being of the horse.

There is nothing more motivating to realize that one day, you will ride well enough to be able to give back to the horses you ride. As your skills develop, your aids will support, redirect, enhance and even improve the horse's natural tendencies. One day, you might notice that your horse is physically healthier and mentally happier because of the riding experiences he receives - from little ol' you!

1. The ultimate release - and the feeling of oneness when everything is going right.

Well, though rarely realized, this togetherness is what will keep you coming back for more. Once you feel the connection, you will be able to persevere through every negative experience, setback and obstacle. Because once you have achieved harmony, you will know why you ride.

Riding toward the ultimate release - this is the stuff riders dream of.

Not the release of the aids - that is a given requirement during all facets of the ride. We ought to regularly create moments of praise/encouragement to the horse during movement through a variety of types of release. We can reward the horse by small gives of the reins, softening the lower back through a movement, a lightening of the leg aids or even just harmonization through the entire body with the horse's motion.

But there is more to the overall scheme of riding than just

the take and release that is required to communicate with the horse.

As you develop in riding, you will come to realize that there is more behind any movement than just the movement itself.

For example, developing a true leg yield can be a task in itself at the beginning. The horse is asked to not only travel straight ahead with a good reach from the hind legs, but then is required to cross the legs over each other while traveling somewhat sideways (but not completely sideways) with that same clear hind end stride. THEN the body must also stay straight - the shoulders cannot lead nor can the hind end.

When you have all these things fall together at the same time, the feeling can be close to euphoric (for both the horse and rider).

However, if you practice leg yields on a regular basis, maintaining the basic correct technique throughout, one day you will be rewarded with a release *from the horse*.

This release is not the one where the horse lightens his pull on your aids, or leans less (although both are by-products). That type of release may happen on a fairly regular basis just through moments of obedience from the horse.

The release I'm talking about is the one where the horse *lets go* in his body. The German terms "losgellasen" and "schwung" (in case you are familiar) combine to describe the process.

We don't really have one English word that matches in meaning, although the closest ones are probably "let loose" and "swing". In effect, the horse releases his tightness within his body (not just the legs). You feel this sudden buoyancy that causes you to imagine you are bouncing on a trampoline.

The strides seem to take longer and reach higher and farther. The bounce in the movement (whichever gait) amplifies, possibly making it more difficult for you to sit through. The movement becomes fluid, expressive, *easy*.

Sometimes, the horse gives you a good snort at this moment, confidently moving forward with enthusiasm but also in balance. Once in a while, you might relish in the appearance of soft, even perhaps floppy ears as the horse finds his "happy place".

As the human partner, you revel in this feel that the horse so generously shares with you. The release of the movement of the horse INSIDE his body gives you a sense of freedom and floating against gravity.

And this is the pinnacle of riding that brings you back time and again.

2 Goals: When Horse Play Becomes Exercise

Horse lovers *love* showing their horses how much they are appreciated.

We do it in all sorts of ways: hand-fed treats, special dinners filled with delicious goodness, or even the extra hug or pat on the neck. We talk to them in soft soothing tones, and we are careful to be extra calm when they are startled by something. We buy them supplements and make sure they get the veterinarian attention they need. Most importantly, we buy well-fitted saddles, properly adjusted bridles, and even get something with a little bling to add that special spark to their overall look.

In our desire to show our horse affection, we lose sight of

one thing - how the horse perceives our actions, and what <u>he</u> would interpret as being a positive interaction.

Of course your horse enjoys your treats, extra nibbles in their feed tub, or your pats and soft-toned voice.

Your horse certainly needs the supplements, vet care and correctly fitting tack to work at his best. And he does need your expert guidance to help him be adequately socialized for this human-dominated environment in which he lives.

But there is one thing that absolutely resonates with your horse on a level that none of the above methods can begin to match - and it's simpler than you can imagine.

The Gift of Exercise

What can make the horse snort, become playfully alert, soft in the eyes and exuberant?

Exercise, of course!

Most horses aren't even particularly picky about what kind of exercise they participate in. Go for a nice trail ride in the woods and smell the crisp outdoor scents. The change of scenery is stimulating as are the sights and sounds of little critters scurrying about doing their daily chores.

Alternately, ride in the ring and work on specific movements. Despite what you may have heard about horses going ring sour through repeated arena riding, you certainly can keep freshness despite doing the same exercises over and over and *over*.

The horse will still relish the fun because working well and moving correctly feels good just as much to him as it does to you.

Not enough time for a full ride? Then enjoy a 20-minute lunging session and work on developing length of stride in all the gaits. How fun can it be? Just look at your horse's face and body language as the minutes roll by and you'll get your answer.

How about a nice bonding session mixed with grooming and a serene hand walking down the driveway of the barn? So many experiences can be shared just by keeping your horse beside you as you go places!

In bad weather, try staying in the barn and playing with a few horse tricks! Tricks are not only physically challenging, but they encourage problem solving and memory work for your favorite equine friend. Even with limited space, you can connect in a way that both you and your horse can enjoy!

The Bottom Line

In this era of horses becoming recreational pets (rather than working livestock), do remember that the horse is hard-wired to move. Nothing pleases him as much as doing what he is supposed to do. Keep it physical, and your horse will appreciate being with *you* more than any horse treat, tack or bling can ever buy!

You never know when a horse chooses to "play"; it can be under saddle or not! The trick is to know how to play along - and use the exuberance for something beneficial.

It is not necessary to only and always ride. There are so many ways to have horsey fun with your favorite equine friend. Just follow his lead and see where it can go. Then put a little goal setting into your play and watch how you can both develop, all the while enjoying each other's company.

Here is a story to show you what I mean.

It's A Good Day For A Little Horse Play

I'm going to let you in on a little secret.

"Playing" can mean anything from riding to trick training to a quick romp together in the field.

When I write for Horse Listening, most of my ideas are sparked by - shall we say - my own "needs". As in, if I need to think about or do something with the horses, I tend to write about it.

We were deep in the throes of winter the day I decided to head out to the barn for a little horseplay. I had been cooped up at work and then in the house for what felt like forever. Add to that the usual daily living demands, and there was little room for horsin' around.

Having said that, the horses don't know the difference. They go out in their paddocks in the morning and come in at night, but in reality, their need for exercise does not diminish even if the footing is off and I stumble in tired from a day's work.

It was a weekend day. The weather was crisp but calm. And there was a fresh covering of snow that was beckoning me to the great outdoors.

As I approached the barn, I could see that the conditions were not the best for a ride. Snow came halfway up my calves, the footing underneath was icy, and the daylight was short.

The sky was blue, the sun was shining and there was no hint of searing winter wind. The weather was just perfect!

Cyrus always enjoys a good grooming session. Unlike the other horses (who tend to be nervous without their buddies), he seems to revel in the attention he gets when he is in the barn all alone. I brushed off the dust from his glossy black coat and finished with soft flicks over his eyes and muzzle. Spending a few moments detangling his tail left him looking almost as pleased as I was about his overall appearance - shiny, midnight black, well muscled despite the lack of exercise, and fluffy tail to top it all off.

I decided to do it the safest way - instead of actually riding, I'd just lunge him. Once in a while, especially after days of no exercise, I might let my horse loose to "free lunge" in the ring, but running loose was not a consideration that day. The outdoor ring was in no condition for me to let my horse go. Although he is pretty street smart about icy footing brought about by wintry conditions, he might nevertheless become over-exuberant and momentarily careless.

I tacked him up like I was going to ride. Saddle pad, saddle and girth, bridle and side reins. With lunge line and whip in hand, we headed off into the snowy winter wonderland that was once our beautiful sandy riding ring in the summer.

I was going to take it easy - just walk around for a while and see what the ground really was like under the snow.

There was no need to be foolish or overly athletic.

Cyrus had other things in mind.

The moment I turned to close the gate, and he saw that he was going to go for a spin, his body outline changed and he radiated horse-language excitement. Time for some fun!

His first few trot steps were a joy to watch. Because the snow went halfway up his cannons, he had to take high, controlled steps, making sparkling new foot holes as he landed in the crisp, clean white snow. Bouncing along, he seemed to spend more time in the air than on the ground, floating along with both grace and power. Sometimes, deep snow can be great for encouraging impulsion!

Soon we got down to business. At first, he trotted carefully while making a path in the snow. He was able to loosen a bit over his back and enjoy the movement more as the snow flattened and became easier to move through.

Then came the snorting session: snort, snort, snort, *snort*! He couldn't tell me in any clearer terms how much he was enjoying the moment.

The footing wasn't so bad after all. He was able to take solid, firm steps and as time went on, he started swinging over the back and taking bolder, longer steps. He stretched his neck down and playfully poked his nose into the snow as he went along, snorting again when the light snow fluffed into his nostrils.

I asked for a little canter. He seemed sure-footed enough, and he looked like he was going to explode with energy! He skipped lightly into the three-beat gait and floated along gracefully as if there was no snow at all. Several snorts later, he broke back into a careful trot, ready to go again at the slightest indication from me.

Then we began to play. Trot - canter - trot. Wow! The trot stride was ever increasing. I think Cyrus is one of the strongest horses I have ever had on a lunge line. He can reach underneath his body with his hind legs deeper than most horses. Where another horse would have problems balancing, he just tilts his croup and his hind legs go pretty much underneath the middle of his body. That way, he seems to have incredibly good control of his power - a little more, and he can change gaits to canter, and a little less, and he can hold his trot stride longer and with surprisingly good balance on a circle.

Today, I thought we could play a little with his trot. He was easily gliding between trot to canter in both directions, so this time, instead of asking for more canter, I asked for a stronger trot without increasing the tempo. I asked him: can you turn up your power without breaking gait or speeding up in the trot and use it instead to reach even further under your body and round your back more?

First, he switched to canter. I asked for a trot and re-established his strong rhythm. The second time I asked for the lengthened strides, he only sped up at the trot. Once again, I slowed the footfalls and resumed the strong trot rhythm.

I tried again. In remarkably little time, he figured it out! When I could see his hind footsteps reaching farther forward than his front footsteps (called "over-tracking"), I was (almost) as excited as he was. He was *loving* the feeling of good movement - I could see it in his eyes, in his bounding steps and enthusiasm, and in his ever-celebratory snorts.

As he finally eased back to a walk, and I began to let his pulse settle through some walk exercises, I realized how possible it really is to spend a little time in movement with your horse even in difficult conditions - and how much the horse appreciates it. As we headed back to the barn, Cyrus walked beside me with dreamy eyes and a softly flowing, calm body.

"Ahh," he seemed to say, "that was nice!"

<u>IN THE RING</u>

Now it is your turn to do something with your horse. Just as in the above story, the conditions might be less than perfect, or your daily life might be impeding in your time with your horse. Yet there can be ways to do something that helps you progress toward your ultimate goals.

So get out there and show your horse how much you care for him!

Take a moment to consider your short and long term goals. What would you like to do today? What would you like to be doing in a year from now? How about five years from now?

Make a plan that can help you and your horse make progress from where you are today to where you want to be in the future!

List the long-term goals and work your way back to the smallest steps you can start with today. Never feel that you have to be tied to these goals - if something comes up along the way, feel free to re-evaluate your progress and fit in the missing parts before you move onto the next level of achievement.

Today, sit down and plan out a regular work schedule for

your horse. Grab a pencil, a calendar or daily planner and write in the answers to these questions.

Long Term Goals

1. What is your dream horse-riding goal? Imagine for a moment that there are no limitations, financially, physically, mentally or horse-wise.

2. What would you like to be doing in five years? This one should be slightly more practical. Be specific.

3. What do you want to be doing in one year? Write out in detail the events you want to participate in, the skills you would like to have achieved, and the supplies/services (i.e. trailering/coaching/ memberships) you will need.

Short Term Goals

1. List the things you need to do and the skills you need within six months from now.

2. List the same as above for one month from now. Pencil in the days you will work your horse during this month.

3. Plan out next week's rides. Know which days you will ride and pick one or two specific skills you would like to do for each ride.

4. Plan out today's riding/training session. Include two specific skills you will work on today.

You don't have to rely on just riding. If you have a round pen, try your hand at getting your horse to respond to you with no tack at all. If you don't have a round pen, consider lunging your horse with side reins, giving him a chance to move without your weight and with a steady rein pressure. Alternately, do some in-hand groundwork.

Even if you have lofty riding goals in the long term, you do not have to ride each and every session with your horse. You can intersperse in saddle days with ground work sessions. Remember that there are many options you have to take on your path to your riding dreams.

One other thing to keep in mind is that you must be always willing to be flexible especially in your short-term goals. If it turns out that your horse is struggling with what you expected to work on today, have the patience and calm frame of mind to go back to what he needs. Address the basics first and then move on to the next steps.

Get out there and enjoy time with your horse!

3 Responsible Horse Ownership

Horses have given us so much since their domestication approximately six thousand years ago.

They gave us power and advantage as cavalry mounts. They carried our wares as pack animals. They pulled our wagons and helped us create new civilizations all over the world. Once we settled, they ploughed our fields and provided us with means to grow food.

Nowadays, horses have taken a back seat to mechanized equipment. They are owned mainly for sport or pleasure, sometimes taking on the role of a pet.

Yet they continue to give.

They give by becoming our companions, our teammates, our recreational pursuits; they help us grow, learn and play. Unfortunately, some are destined to misfortune due to ignorance or greed.

Many of us feel like it is our turn to give back. However, we need to keep in mind that horses are prey animals and long-time domesticated livestock. If we listen well enough, we discover that what we think of as giving might not be what the horses truly need.

As owners of these magnificent animals, it is our responsibility to prepare them for a life within the environment and structure in which we live.

By taking on horse ownership, we are taking on the duty of caring for and training our horses in such a way that enables them to survive well in our social structures.

In other words, our horses should be trained sufficiently and suitably socialized to do well in a human-ized environment. Unless we can buy 20,000 acres (or more) of pastureland with plenty of natural resources to support a herd of untouched (wild) horses, it becomes our duty to help our horses know how to get by in this world of the human.

Some examples

Our horses should not bite. They should not walk over or kick their handlers. They should allow people to interact with them in a way that keeps people safe from harm.

And it falls to us to teach them socially appropriate behavior, because the bottom line is that if the horse does *not* respond appropriately in regard to humans, he will be the one that suffers in the long run - and potentially be put down.

In the end, the horse will always take the blame for any inadequacies in behavior and suffer the consequences.

How to Be A Responsible Horse Owner

It behooves us to carefully step into horse ownership with as much knowledge as possible. We must surround ourselves with a solid support system of friends, barn managers, riding instructors and equine professionals such as veterinarians to teach us, guide us, correct us when needed, and be our horse's human representatives. It truly does take a herd of many to support each horse - whether a horse herd or a human herd!

It takes a lot more to be a responsible horse owner than just providing green grass for horses to graze on (although that is certainly an important factor in the horse's health and well-being).

There are so many aspects of responsible horse ownership:
- simple horse training of day-to-day tasks.

- bringing a horse along carefully and compassionately as a young horse.

- having an intrinsic lifelong passion for learning all things "horse" (the desire for self-improvement).

- representing a horse honestly and ethically when presenting him for sale.

- teaching people who are new to horses in a similarly responsible manner, even if they have (possibly misguided) ideas of their own.

Whether you own a foal, a young horse or an old-timer, always be aware of your responsibility to your horse. Being a good horse listener and responsible owner means that you get to "give back" in a way that ensures a long and comfortable life for your horse.

4 Nine Things You Need To Know If You Want To Ride Horses

You might have liked horses all your life. Or you might have had an awakening not too long ago that is urging you to explore horseback riding for the first time. You can't tear your eyes away from the sight of glowing coats and rippling muscles. You get excited every time you drive by horses in a field.

Contrary to your friends, you even like the smell of a barn!

And now, you know you are ready to take the first steps on the long road of becoming an equestrian. You've booked riding lessons at a local barn and you are convinced that you are ready to tackle the learning curve that lays ahead.

Before you begin, here are nine tips to smooth the way into your new adventures!

1. Be prepared to be a beginner - for a long time!

Once you step into that stirrup for the first time, forget all about instant gratification. Instead, get all pumped up for the accomplishment of doing something for the long term.

Don't worry if your fingers fumble when putting on the bridle. Have no worry when the horse gives you a knowing look out of the corner of his eye: "This one is a beginner!"

Just take the plunge into new feels, new learning curves and new coordination. It's all about the joys (and challenges) of being on the path.

2. Every horse has something to teach you.

If you ride at a riding school, and have had the chance to ride many horses over the course of a few years, you will truly understand that there is something to be learned from every horse you ride.

If you part-board or lease a horse, you can have the opportunity to work with one horse over the long term. You might develop a deeper relationship and maybe even know each other so well that you can read each other's minds.

But always be appreciative of the chance to ride new horses because they will add to your depth of experience and repertoire of "language" you need to ride effectively.

3. Find an excellent mentor.

Your mentor might or might not be your instructor. However, this person will be critical to the success of your first years as a horse rider.

She will be the one who can listen to your questions and concerns and give you the answers you need for your situation.

She will guide you in your decisions and help you find the

solutions that are necessary for your development - even if you are not aware of them at the time. Find someone you can trust.

4. Surround yourself with great professionals and horse friends.

It is true that you are the sum of the influences around you. So search for people you admire and look up to. Find the ones who you would like to emulate. Then, be around them and learn from them at every opportunity.

Get to know the professionals in your area - from nutrition, to health care, to training - it is essential for you to be surrounded by kind, compassionate people who always put the horse first when they make decisions.

5. Although the initial learning seems quick and easy, don't despair once your learning curve seems to slow down.

At some point, your riding skills will plateau and try as you might, new learning becomes frustrating and difficult. Be ready for that time period and be willing to keep trudging through - until you reach your next series of leaps and bounds.

However, the plateaus will always reappear, just before the next real learning curve; they are just a fact of life.

6. Be ready to be physical in a way you've never experienced before.

Riding is like no other sport because of the presence of the horse. Rubbing your belly and chewing gum is an easy task compared to riding!

In order to truly move with the horse, you have to learn to coordinate body parts you never knew you had, and then *also* stay on top of a moving 1,000 pound animal! But have no fear - it will all come together in the long run.

7. Watch, read, study, do.

It goes without saying that there is much learning to be done off the horse's back. Read books to study what the movements should be like. Watch videos of professionals and even amateurs (especially now that videos are so easily accessible on the Internet). Go to clinics and watch how other riders develop under the eye of an experienced clinician. Then take your own lessons, go to clinics and shows or video yourself. Use every available means to solicit feedback.

Then study some more!

8. Be wary of the "a little knowledge is a dangerous thing" stage.

This happens to everyone at least once in their riding career. There eventually comes a time, once you have made your mistakes and learned from them, that you begin to feel pretty confident about your equine-related skills. The tack no longer defies you. You develop the balance and coordination needed to walk, trot and canter without feeling like you might fall off any second. You can even ride and talk at the same time!

When it all starts to come together like this, you might become a little more confident than were at the beginning. You start to take more riding risks. You might think about changing routines to suit yourself better - change the barn, or ditch your instructor!

Before you head off into the land of grass is greener everywhere else, heed these words! You will want to spread your wings and fly - that is a fact. However, although there are certainly many ways to Rome, especially in the equine world, don't "instructor hop". Nothing is more confusing than trying to comprehend different people's systems over and over again.

9. Listen to your horse.

Although it sounds a little far-fetched, it is indeed possible to "hear" your horse if you understand their routines, structures and communications. If life is good, your horse will show you his pleasure by becoming more rideable. He will be calm but at the same time responsive to you. He will improve his ground manners, develop consistency under saddle, and work with you toward a better partnership.

If, on the other hand, he becomes less receptive, more difficult to handle, and lose overall condition, you will know this is not the path you want to be on. Just listen and then make decisions according to the feedback.

Well, there you have it! Hopefully, these tips will help you as you progress from newbie to old-timer!

Just when you think you know something, you realize there is so much more you need to know.

5 Five Reasons Why It Takes Two People To Ride One Horse

They say two is better than one.

In horseback riding, nothing can be truer.

It's not that two people should ride the horse - well, unless you want to do that too. It's more about how the efforts of two people combine to make to make the riding experience better for the horse - as well as the rider.

There is no replacement for an educated eye on the ground. Add willingness, compassion and resourcefulness to your ground person, and almost every riding situation can be improved thanks to both your efforts. The ground person might be your instructor or not. The prerequisite is that you both work toward the same goal, one from the back of the horse, and the other from the ground.

Here are five reasons why two people are better than one.

1. Calm the horse and/or the rider.

Has this ever happened to you? Your ride has been going just fine. Then, after passing the same corner of the arena multiple times, your horse decides that his life will end the next time he heads over there. At that moment, your trusty ground person walks over to the corner and protects your horse just by standing there and using a calm tone of voice as you ride by.

The ground person can also be your calming factor. If you feel anxious, unsure or tentative, the ground person can be an excellent source of information and inspiration - the type that reassures and challenges at each turn. If you feel confident, your person can push you to reach higher goals, encouraging you to step just that little bit out of your comfort zone.

2. Increase impulsion.

Your ground person can also be a motivator to help your horse put in that missing bit of "oomph" needed to complete a movement. Although the rider can do much from the horse's back to achieve impulsion and engagement, many horses respond nicely to a ground person. The right body language and verbal cues given in the right moment might be all that is needed to gently coax the horse into working more from the hind end.

3. Set up and take down equipment.

This is when the ground person is irreplaceable! If a person is willing to move equipment during your ride, you can be free to train your horse rather than worry about getting off to readjust things.

The ground person can re-set anything that was knocked down or pushed over while you negotiated the obstacle. She can change the level of difficulty as your horse develops the confidence after several repetitions. She can change patterns according to how the ride is going.

4. Give visual feedback.

One of the difficulties of riding (especially without mirrors) is that while you ride, you receive very little visual feedback. While you can see the head and neck of the horse, everything behind you is limited to your ability to feel results. The ground person can be the visual feedback you are missing. She can let you know if you and your horse are straight, if the movement you tried was successful, and what your horse looks like. She can let you in on details such as if your horse is crossing the legs in the leg yield or if the halt was square. Of course you should be able to feel such things eventually, but getting that immediate feedback can help develop your accurate feel and prevent problems from occurring in the first place.

5. Motivate each other.

Sparks fly when two motivated people have a chance to "bounce off" one another! When one person has an idea, the other can take it to another level by adding their piece to it. The same thing can happen when riding horses. Problem-solving becomes easier, brainstorming is quicker, the energy is enthusiastic and positive. One idea leads to another and soon enough, goals are reached and obstacles are overcome.

When two people ride one horse, the whole environment changes. Teamwork is useful in all aspects of life, but when done effectively during a ride, the horse is the one that benefits. And the horse's well-being should always be our primary intention.

Section 2: The Essentials

6 Six Ways to Unleash the Power of Your Seat

The seat is the foundation of all riding, regardless of discipline.

First, there are hands and legs. When we learn to ride, we tend to guide the horse primarily through the use of our hands, then through our legs. Rein aids and leg aids reign supreme (pun intended!): left rein here, right rein there, inside leg, outside leg... you know the routine. And without a doubt, it is essential to learn the use of hands and legs to achieve a basic sense of control of the horse - it is not always a pleasant experience to have a spirited equine expressing his enthusiasm while you hang on for dear life!

As you become subtler in the aiding process, you will begin to discover just how powerful the seat can be.

As time goes on, however, you begin to develop a sense for the horse's balance, for the energy that moves through the body, and for the 'release' that the horse can achieve given the opportunity. You begin to develop 'feel' through your seat. When is the horse lifting/dropping his back? When are the hind legs underneath the body? How much energy is needed to allow just enough 'forward' for the horse to reach but not so much that he will fall to the forehand?

As you become subtler in the aiding process, you will begin to discover just how powerful the seat can be in guiding the horse without disturbing and interfering in his movement.

1. Find Your Seat.

Get yourself a good instructor that knows how to teach the finer points of using the seat during riding. There are a lot of people who use their seat effectively but for one reason or another cannot seem to be able to explain well enough to break it down into achievable skills. You must learn how to activate your seat bones, and differentiate between using the seat versus weight aids.

Developing control of the "inner" components of the seat will take time and perseverance, as this is likely not a typical movement that you're used to. Look at it as a 2-year goal - one that takes thousands of repetitions to master.

Lunging on a reliable, rhythmical school horse might be on the menu in order to allow you to free your lower back, hips and thighs enough to begin to feel the physical requirements of using your seat.

Know that it is extremely worthwhile to put that much effort into the skill acquisition, as everything, including your balance, revolves around an effective use of the seat.

2. Develop Effective Half-halts.

The seat is a key component to a half-halt. Without the seat, your half-halt is about as effective as a pull from your hand, or a kick from the leg. Neither aids really help the horse in rebalancing, which is the ideal result desired from the half-halt. Use your seat to keep your horse "with" you - brace your lower back to rebalance the horse's momentum and weight to the hind end.

Use your seat bones laterally to allow half-halts to effect one side only (horse leaning on one side, or drifting through a shoulder) and alternately, use diagonal half-halts (inside seat bone to outside supporting rein) to encourage better use of the hind end by the horse.

3. Free Your Seat to Free the Horse's Back.

Encourage your horse to move "forward"- rather than use your legs to kick a horse onward, use your seat to encourage the more balanced sense of being 'forward'.

In the trot, you can follow along with the horse in a more giving way through your entire seat, opening on the "up" phase of the posting trot (without actually posting).

Your seat has the power to encourage the horse to "step through" with its hind legs and develop a lovely rhythmical swinging of the back ("schwung") that will allow for a willing and supple response to your aids.

4. Transition From the Seat.

Rather than using your hands for a downward transition, or your legs for an upward transition, use your seat as the "root" to the transition - either upward or downward. Move your seat into the next gait (even if it is a downward transition) and expect the horse to respond almost entirely off your seat aid. Use hands/legs only if absolutely necessary, after you applied the seat aid. Be ready to reinforce the seat aid but don't use it if it is not required. Always use as much as needed but only as much as necessary.

5. Change Directions.

Did you know that you can allow a horse to turn smoothly and in balance simply from a seat aid? Your hands work on keeping the horse straight through the turn, and your seat works from the waist down to turn the horse from his middle.

Soon you will be free from "steering" the horse with your hands. Eventually, the horse will appear to read your mind because the aids will become incredibly subtle and shared only between you and your horse. The only visible result will be the lack of fuss and a total unison in movement.

6. Stop (No Hands Needed)!

After a series of half-halts, it will only take your seat to stop the horse's legs. Simply stop moving and "halt" with your seat. Remember to keep your legs on as the horse still needs to complete the halt by bringing his legs underneath him.

Your thought process could go like this: "bring your (hind) legs under, bring your legs under, bring your legs under, halt."

The above ideas are just the beginning. Use your seat to do lateral work such as shoulder-in, haunches-in, walk or canter pirouettes, half-passes and flying changes.

Start to feel the effects of your seat and learn to communicate with the horse from the middle rather than the front. The more you learn about and activate your seat, the more you will discover about the incredible power of the seat.

7 Why You Don't Want to Pull on the Inside Rein - and What To Do Instead

When we ride horses, we often assume that the inside rein is used like the steering wheel of a car or a bicycle. We think that by pulling on the horse from the inside, the horse must obviously turn his nose and then follow it. Right?

Pulling to Turn

In some cases, the turn does happen. The horse's body moves along the direction of the head and he accommodates us the best he can. This is the reason why many of us think we are on the right track by pulling to turn.

However, at some point in time, we begin to better understand the biomechanics of pulling and how it affects the horse's body.

Sometimes, although the horse certainly turns his nose in the direction of the pull, his body continues in the original trajectory. He doesn't easily make the turn. Other times, his body even goes in the *opposite direction* (in effect, drifting out) from where we pointed his nose! Has this ever happened to you?

Then we learn about the usefulness of the outside rein in turns. We practice using the outside rein while turning until it eventually becomes a habit.

But there is one other consequence to pulling on that inside rein that has little to do with turning. It isn't as straightforward to identify or visualize. And it affects the horse under almost every circumstance - on a turn, over a straight line, in a gait change, through a half-halt and more.

Blocking the Inside Hind Leg

If you want to prevent the inside hind leg from coming through underneath the body, here is how you do it: *pull back on the inside rein.*

The only problem is that the haunches then cannot support the horse's balance. Without the hind end as the engine, the horse is left to having to initiate movement from his front legs. He must then drag his body (and yours) along from the front, thus losing balance and falling to the forehand. You know the rest: tripping, stumbling, tension, rock-hard hollow back, discomfort and so on.

What NOT To Do

Most people's reaction is to do the exact opposite and fully drop the inside rein. Sometimes, you can even see the droop as if the rider wants to say, "See? I don't even have any contact at all!"

Having absolutely no contact can be counterproductive too, because then there is no way for you to support the horse when necessary.

You will end up with an on-again, off-again contact that becomes difficult for the horse to negotiate. In the end, no contact can be as bad as too much contact.

There is always a happy medium.

What To Do

You have three strategies.

#1 is the easiest to do while #3 takes the most coordination. You can probably progress through the steps as you become better able to find that release. Your horse might also have a preference between the three at different times - so you can use the skill that suits him best in the moment.

Please note: these techniques can be used in the same manner on a snaffle bit (short rein length) or any curb/shank bit (long rein length) or anything in-between! Please feel free to try this in your riding style and discipline.

1. You could let out an inch of rein.

Lengthening the rein an inch out (2cm or so for those of us using the metric system!) might be all the horse needs to get the freedom in the hind quarters. The rein is therefore short enough for us to communicate with him at a moment's notice, but long enough that there is that space for him to reach - from his hind legs, over his topline and through the poll to the bit.

There is no better feeling than when the horse *reaches* for the bit into the rein space you just gave him!

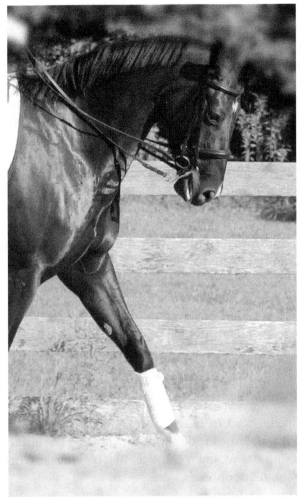

Here, I have let out an inch or so of rein.

2. You could maintain the same rein length and let out your elbow.

This strategy gives the horse the same feeling as #1 but you don't need to let out the rein length. When is it useful to maintain the same rein length?

When you know you need to be able to give clear and timely half-halts in order to help the horse maintain balance through a variety of movements. For example, if your instructor is asking you to negotiate several movements in sequence, you won't have the time to let the rein out and take it back, and doing so will unnecessarily disrupt your horse's balance.

Instead, you just let your elbows out and take them back in the following strides. The effect is the same - the horse gets a release and then a take-up for further communication.

3. You could move better with the horse with the same rein and contact pressure.

This one is the icing on the cake.

If you can move through your *entire body*, staying in sync with the horse's movements but releasing where and when needed, you will have one happy, confident, bold moving horse.

You might need to release through your seat. You might "loosen" through the inside shoulder, allowing the inside hind to reach within a moment's notice. Maybe your legs need to "breathe" with your horse's sides.

In any case, riding in tandem with the horse is something we always aspire to and there is good reason for that. When you both move "as one", the earth stops rotating and you float on that ninth cloud!

Letting the inside hind leg do its job is one of the first keys to riding with the horse in mind!

8 What Do Leg Aids Mean?

The leg aids are one of the most basic, "natural" aids we have to communicate with the horse. All riders regularly use their legs to give messages to the horse, but most of the time, the legs mean go faster or change gait.

Fortunately, there are many other uses for leg aids. Using them for the "go" message is good to use when you are a novice rider and beginning to grapple with the various aids. However, as you develop your skills, your aids can evolve to become less intrusive and more specific. Instead of relying on them only to get the horse to move his legs faster or transition to a new gait, we might discover more involved messages that can be given with a sophisticated leg aid.

Although there are many variations of how to use your legs, we will discuss their *purpose* in this article. Also, the other aids (weight, hands, seat bones) must be employed along with the legs for all movements, but here we will look only at the legs.

What the leg aids do not mean:

Gait change.

Riders are taught early in their education that the legs should be positioned in particular ways to indicate gait change. While this is an effective method to communicate a particular gait to a horse, riders often confuse the two leg kick as a gait change. Soon enough, the horse thinks, "upward transition" to any leg use.

It might seem that a quick change of gaits is desirable. However, what you miss out on by letting the horse "leak" into the next gait is the opportunity to allow the horse to use his back and engage within a gait.

To get a fluid gait change, use your leg positions but initiate the movement with your seat.

Tempo change.

Changing leg speed is somewhat related to the gait change above. If the horse can't change gaits in response to leg, then surely it must go faster within the gait! The problem is that by allowing the horse to go faster faster faster, you suddenly find yourself on the forehand and out of balance. Half-halts become difficult to do and you often have to resort to pulling the horse to slow down and regain balance.

Once again, regulate the tempo with your seat.

Pain.

People often feel that it is necessary to use strong kicking legs.

The leg aid is used for many different purposes. Here it is softly draping along the horse's side at the girth.

Kicking is unfair if it is being used to inflict pain. Just as with any other aid, legs (and spurs) should be used as a method of communication and not for causing discomfort or distress to the horse.

What they do mean:

Go (impulsion)!

Leg aids tell the horse to step deeper underneath the body with the hind legs. There might or might not be a gait change involved. However, the leg speed should not change nor should the gait change be initiated solely by the legs.

The legs aids may result in a slight whiplash effect for the rider as the horse engages the hind end and creates a stronger, more active stride. This is good!

Reach for the bit (longitudinal flexion).

Two legs can encourage a horse to lift his back. Along with impulsion, the horse can learn to allow the energy over the topline so that the back will lift, round and therefore the horse can reach forward to the bit.

Bend (lateral flexion).

Stepping away from the leg aid allows the horse to bend "through" the rib cage. The space that is created by a sideways shift of the ribs allows the horse to bring the inside hind leg deeper under the body. This is often helpful for the horse to balance better through turns and corners. These leg aids are also useful for shoulder-in and haunches-in.

Step away (lateral movement).

The leg aid that lingers is asking the horse to step away in a lateral manner. These leg aids are used for movements such as leg yields, half-pass and full pass (a.k.a. side pass).

Bear in mind that the legs are just a part of the overall

communication process that goes into aiding the horse. If we are clear on why we use leg aids, the "how" becomes easier and makes more sense.

9 An Active Stretch Versus the Neck Down

The active stretch helps to release the horse's topline and often helps the horse find his "happy place".

Ode To The Stretchy Trot

Oh stretchy trot, friend of friends,
honest and true,
how do I love thee?
Let me count the ways.

There in the beginning,
and there at the end,
thy calming presence
evolving into the finest equine dance.

Compulsory test circle
or ultimate personal choice,
available at a moment's notice,
thou art the true collaborator.

Releasing tension, transmitting serenity
to the mind,
encouraging relaxation,
improving weight carriage;
Steadfastly the soothing one during
tumultuous times.

.

I know when thou art here:
soft ears, loose muscles, bounciness,
floating light-stepped-ness,
and
the ever-pervasive snorts!

.

Not a mere "neck down"
or some prescribed posture to behold,
thou art an overall body stretch
through the topline from tail to ear.

59

> I cannot express
> enough love for thee,
> save that I will be here, lingering,
> eagerly awaiting your next appearance.

*****

Developing the skills to encourage an effective stretchy trot might not be as easy as it looks. The horse that has never reached forward and down might not be particularly enthusiastic to try in the beginning, and for good reason.

The horse's field of vision might change significantly when the head is low to the ground. Since his vision becomes compromised, he has to put more trust into his rider.

Be the leader that he is looking for (through confident, calm riding) so he might take the initial risks.

Stretching over the topline might also lull the horse into calmness - but many horses confuse calm with inactivity. Be sure to encourage strong, forward strides especially when the horse reaches down with the neck.

In the beginning, if I could get the horse to drop his head even just below the withers, I thought I was getting a beginner sort of stretch. I was so pleased that I could influence the horse enough to get him to drop his neck.

Then as time went on, and with my ever-patient instructor at my side, I realized that just getting the horse to drop his neck actually had nothing to do with getting a stretch.
Why not?

Well, that was my burning question after about a month (or more!) of neck-downs and still no *real* stretch!

The Passive Stretch

In reality, the passive stretch is not really a stretch. It is more of a what I now think of as a "neck-down". The catch is that many people cannot tell the difference between a passive versus an active stretch, and therefore get caught in the passive conundrum without even knowing it.

When you are new to getting your horse to stretch, you don't know what a truly active stretch feels like. Initially, it can even be a little overwhelming to watch the horse as his neck goes down, down, down, seemingly into a never-ending abyss. It can even become a little uncomfortable to feel the imbalance the neck-down may cause, since the horse does in fact fall to the forehand in a passive stretch.

The neck-down is initiated by the reins. You learn that if you take the contact long enough, the horse will start looking for a release.

At one point, the horse will drop his head and you will release. And so - as with anything (right?) - take more contact and the horse will quickly learn to drop his head even lower. Your release at the bottom will reinforce that he did the right thing.

And then your superstar fantastic instructor tells you that you are NOT doing a stretch!

Problems

After many, many more tries, you might start to discover

that the problem with the passive stretch is that it is merely a posture. Similar to reaching down for grass, the horse learns to reach down for the pressure release.

If the back was hollow before the neck going down, it will still be hollow. If the horse wasn't properly using his hind end, the disengagement will continue and might even become more pronounced.

At the walk, it might not be much of a problem. At the trot, you can begin to really feel the horse leaning to the forehand. If you try a neck-down at the canter, you will really know what imbalance feels like! Beware - the horse may fall to the forehand enough to slip or trip.

The Active Stretch

The active stretch is different in so many ways.

1. It starts from the hind end. The key is that there should be movement. Without impulsion from the hind end, there will be no stretch.

2. The energy travels over the topline, and *because* of that energy, the horse reaches forward to the bit. If the horse is being truly energetic - from the rear - he will spontaneously want to round, release the tension in the topline and begin the stretch. You should feel a surge of energy (I think of it as a mild whip-lash effect), which ends in the horse's desire to reach forward and down. How far he reaches forward and down depends on the depth of your release.

3. Finally, the major difference is that **your release of the reins** encourages the horse to reach down even more. Therefore, other than the original level of contact, there is no more taking up of rein or tightening or pulling or moving your elbows backward.

During and After the Stretch

The other major difference between the active and passive stretch is level of activity. While the horse is stretching, he is still *with* you. In the passive stretch, you effectively drop the horse and let go. Then, you must "take up" again (your reins, contact, energy, connection).

In the active stretch, you are still present through the whole movement. You can half-halt through your seat and reins, you can use your leg aids and you can smoothly resume the usual riding outline once the stretch is over.

The reins are not loopy, or completely released.

There is always a light, effective contact between you and your horse, regardless of where the head and neck is.

Begin to Float

You will know when you have found the active stretch. There is simply no comparison to the neck-down. You will feel:

- the horse's energy surge

- the back actually becoming rounder and stronger

- the strides become larger and bolder

- the body loosen up, the horse become enthusiastic and calm at the same time, and just this overall buoyancy that wasn't there with the neck down.

Combine all the above and you will begin to float, equine-style!

IN THE RING

Try several approaches to the stretchy trot:

1) Use it as part of your warm-up.

Some horses benefit a great deal from a topline release early in their ride. It settles them mentally and frees them physically.

2) Stretch on a circle.

It is generally easier to stretch when the horse is bent on a circle. The bend encourages an horse's hind leg to reach further forward to help in balance and control. It also helps to contain the horse without having to pull on the reins.

Go to a straight line stretch only when you have attained a secure rhythm and half-halts that "go through" without the use of reins.

3) Use half-halts.

Just because the reins are long doesn't mean that you can let the horse flop into on-the-forehand heaven! A series of strategically placed half-halts will help your horse keep his balance to the hind end, which will in turn allow him to release his topline even more.

Good luck, and happy stretching!

10 Stepping "Forward" in Horseback Riding

The term 'forward' is used liberally in horse riding but can often be misunderstood. We tend to think a horse is forward when the legs are moving and the horse is flying along - but this picture is far from the truth. So if forward is not an increase in tempo (the speed of the footfalls), then what is it?

Imagine a mother/father and child walking along holding hands. There can be several variations in this scene:

- both parent and child are walking along in tandem, progressing through space at a mutually accepted pace, willingly and confidently reaching for each other's hand.

- the child is pulling ahead of the parent, thereby pulling the parent off his/her feet.

- the child is pulling behind the parent, thereby causing the parent to slow down/stop.

- the child is pulling sideways from the parent but the parent isn't letting go; this causes the parent to be dragged left/right, again causing a disturbance in the progression.

The only 'forward' scenario is the first. The parent and child move along in tandem while holding hands, matching stride for stride and walking/running in a cooperative, mutually beneficial manner.

Similarly, when a horse is 'forward', it is reaching ahead of itself, gamely assuming a forward space each stride, reaching confidently to the bit, and showing a calm, confident, round and overall happy and willing demeanor. The horse can reach forward for the bit in the same way that a child offers his hand to be taken.

Of course, the hand of the rider must be as accepting and gentle as the hand of the parent, inspiring the horse to want to reach even more and settle into a comfortable "happy place."

A Forward Horse Looks Calm and Enthusiastic

A horse can be forward while slowly progressing through space - so speed is not a variable in being forward. In fact, a horse can be moving backward and still be 'forward'! Confused yet?!

Even though being 'forward' is primarily a secretly hidden feeling kept between the horse and rider, you actually can *see* 'forward'.

What does it look like?

- The horse is round, calm and athletic looking: it appears as though the horse can stop/turn/change gait at a moment's notice.

- The horse has soft (not pinned to a scary object), forward ears; it looks like he is eagerly moving to somewhere he wants to go.

- The hind legs freely reach deep underneath the body (as far as conformation allows).

- There is a sense of graceful power; the horse can float into upward or downward transitions without losing balance.

- The horse is *off* the forehand; he is neither heavy on the hands and heading into the ground nor is he hollow-backed with a 'giraffe neck' sticking upward at an awkward angle.

- The tempo of the gait is strong, powerful, supple and almost leisurely - there is no scrambling for speed nor does the horse look like it's stuck in quicksand.

- Most importantly, the horse looks to be comfortable, confident and enjoying the moment.

Realistically speaking, we spend most of our riding time NOT being in a forward state. Many factors contribute to a horse being 'backward' including rushing/being lazy, scary spots (spooking), distractions, uneven footing, and even the mood of the horse or the rider. In fact, being forward results in an improved psychological and physical state - for both the rider and the horse.

How can you develop a "forward" state in your ride? Here is one example. One of the easiest and most beneficial solutions to many riding problems is to teach the horse to move from the hind end.

Why do we harp so much on this topic?

Simply put, everything starts with impulsion. Impulsion starts with the hind end.

Every horse benefits from stepping deeper with the hind end.

If the stride is longer, the hind legs can reach further underneath the body and support the horse's balance with more strength and agility.

The energy derived from the increased impulsion can then travel over the back (topline) allowing for better carriage of the rider and a loftier, bouncier movement, whether it is walk, trot or canter. It can help to straighten the horse. It can resolve "behavior" issues. It can even help to reduce tension in the horse's body.

How to Increase Impulsion

For the horse that does not typically, or naturally, use the hind end, taking two deeper steps might be difficult at first. He might translate the request to mean that he has to move his legs faster, or fall to the inside/outside, or change the gait entirely.

You might have to coordinate your "go" request with an immediate "no" to help him rebalance rather than to scramble underneath that extra energy.

All it takes is two stronger steps, in the same gait, in the same rhythm, tempo and direction. Use two squeezing calf leg aids with a corresponding seat aid for "forward." You may need a half-halt (or two) following the energy surge.

In other words, ask for increased energy but:

- don't let the horse get faster in the gait.

- don't let the horse change gaits.

- don't let the horse scramble because of the extra energy

- stop him from falling to the forehand.

- help him send the energy straight forward (avoid letting him become crooked).

Teach him to use that burst of energy to lengthen the stride of his hind legs.

You know you are on the right track when:

- the stride becomes bouncier.

- the stride feels longer (you travel over more ground with less steps).

- you feel less overall tension in the horse's body.

- the horse goes straighter (doesn't gall to the inside or outside on a turn or line).

- you get more "air time."

- the horse begins to round (without you pulling on the reins).

- the footfalls are lighter when the horse lands.

The "forward" horse is naturally round in outline and deeply engaged with the hind leg.

- for geldings, the sheath sound disappears.

- the horse gives you a heartfelt snort!

<u>IN THE RING</u>

Identifying the "forward" state takes practice and a knowledgeable eye on the ground. Ask your instructor (or well educated friend) to catch you in the act of being "forward."

Work for it regularly, get help in identifying when your horse is forward and memorize how it feels. Then challenge yourself. Be "forward" during these times:

1) A Circle

Many horses tend to relax (as in, go on vacation) on a circle. If you do not regularly ask for engagement as you go around the circle, you will notice the horse slows tempo, shortens stride and generally looks lazy. This is normal!

It is up to you to stay vigilant and not lose your forward feel as you complete the circle.

2) Coming to the rail or corner of the ring.

Horses almost always "suck back" when approaching a wall. Be a responsible rider and ask your horse to maintain his energy and deep hind end stride as you approach the wall or corner. Have a slight bend in the direction you are going and give the horse somewhere to go other than the wall. Then rev the engine!

3) Misbehavior

Did you know that almost all behavior concerns stem from lack of forward? Prevent rears, bucks, kicks and deek-outs to the side by providing straight and forward guidance before the behavior is evident.

The next time you run into tension, leaning, drifting, hollow back or many of the other problems that we often think of as resistance or reluctance, try this simple technique. Ask for just two steps of increased energy. Then, evaluate. If you feel there could be more, ask for another two steps.

And see what your horse thinks about it.

11 Go and No

Without forward, there is no half-halt but without half-halt, there is no forward.

Let me explain.

Has it ever happened to you that after you kicked (or preferably, *didn't* kick but used more seat/leg for more energy), the horse flew out from under you, running faster and faster until he fell to the forehand and perhaps had to scramble his way back to balance?

Or conversely...

Has it ever happened that you went to half-halt and the horse braced his neck against your pressure, slowed the rhythm and reduced energy until you thought you were stuck in quicksand?

In both cases, there is one aid given to the horse but the other is missing. And there seems to be no other way: if you want to control energy, you have to have energy in the first place. If there is no energy, there is no controlling.

What to do?

We have to learn the coordination between "go and no" - all the while, keeping our balance to give the appropriate aids while not pulling on the reins.

Teach your horse to kick (not literally!) into gear when you use a light leg and encouraging seat (that floats right into the movement that your horse offers). Then, before it's too late and he loses balance completely, use a restricting seat, contact with your (probably outside) rein, and a little leg to help the horse's hind end to come underneath his body.

See if he steps deeper underneath his body, rounds more, becomes bouncier, and breathes deeper (or gives you a well-earned snort). Look for more swing in his stride, more reach through his shoulders, and a lighter contact pressure on the reins.

The rhythm should be unaffected. A half-halt is a rebalance; it isn't a "putt-er down into the slower gait little by little and let the energy peter out."

Therefore, the idea isn't to interfere with the horse's gait and tempo. Instead, your aim is to celebrate the energy your horse gives you and redirect it not only straight forward, but also a little upward, so the overall balance tilts a little to the hind end.

There has to be a balance between energy input and control so that the horse can maintain his balance through turns and all other movements.

<u>IN THE RING</u>

Keep your balance.
Encourage more energy.
Keep the tempo constant (not faster or slower).
Get the "go", then get the "no".
Do it on a straight line.
Then do it on a circle.

12 A Question of Imbalance: Can You Tell?

We often obsess over riding in balance or the lack thereof. We deliberate on the techniques we can use to resume balance - or better yet, *stay* in balance. But before we can problem-solve and correct, we need to know that the horse did, in fact, lose balance in the first place.

In the beginning, it is difficult to feel the difference. As time goes on and you develop new "nerve endings" (not literally - it's just that you become more sensitive to certain feelings or situations), you begin to differentiate between being in and out of balance.

It takes time and practice because each horse has his own way of going. Add specific conformation and it's no wonder that it might take several years to identify the nuances that point to imbalance in the horse you are riding.

There are as many solutions as there are reasons why a horse has lost balance. For the purposes of this article, we are going to focus on how you can identify an imbalance. We hope the list will assist especially those who new to riding, or to those who do not have professional help while they ride.

It is sometimes easier to notice a balanced horse while watching instead of riding, But at some point, it becomes essential to be able to *feel* what is happening so that you can hopefully address it sooner than later.

A trip or stumble.

When horses lose balance, they tend to fall forward-downward in response to the pull of gravity. Thanks to their four legs, they rarely actually fall to the ground (under normal riding conditions). If you have a horse that trips or stumbles often, you might consider that he is being ridden off balance.

A tightening of the back.

Ever felt a back that reminds you of a plywood board? Horses that fall out of balance often have to tighten their backs to compensate for the being on the forehand.

Jarring sitting trot.

Youch! Along with the plywood back, the trot becomes stiffer and stiffer until it becomes very difficult to sit to. Guess what? This is another sign that your horse is off balance.

Lack of movement.

Sometimes it is easy to think that a small moving horse is a good moving horse. We often think that not moving feels good (because we don't have to work as hard to stay with the horse). However, the horse must rely on his hind legs to support the weight of the forehand, and lack of stride length is a major contributor to imbalance.

Sewing-machine trot.

We've talked about this one before. The horse that trots faster faster faster is without a doubt out of balance.

Runaway canter.

The same goes for the canter. Horses that have difficulty making downward transitions, or half-halts within a gait, are often out of balance.

"Hard mouth."

We can mistake what feels like a reluctant poll or hard mouth for disobedience when it is in fact the horse trying to manage his lack of balance as he moves along.

Inconsistent contact.

Have you ever felt your reins go on-and-off even though you tried hard to maintain a steady contact?

The cause may be the horse coming out of balance rather than just your rein length or pressure.

Unresponsiveness.

An imbalanced horse has more difficulty responding to aids. He tends to scramble and save himself but he might not be able to do what you want him to be doing.

"Giraffe neck."

This is a term for a neck position that many horses carry. The neck protrudes out of the body in an awkward angle, low at the base of the neck and high at the poll. The giraffe neck is usually stiff and it may be difficult to get the horse to bend or look in the direction of travel.

Drifting to the outside.

The horse that moves against your outside aids and heads to the rails sideways is already out of balance.

Tight, falling to the inside turn or circle.

The opposite is also true! Many horses turn sharp into one direction, making tiny circles or tight, uncontrolled turns.

Horse traveling up the rail with the head and neck pointing to the wall.

Take a look next time you go up the rail. Does your horse "lean in" diagonally with the haunches pointing to the middle of the ring? Then he is off balance.

Lack of straightness.

This goes hand in hand with the diagonally-moving horse. Any type of lack of straightness (i.e. shoulder jutting out, horse leaning heavily on your leg, etc.) contributes to lack of balance. The question now may be, what to do about the loss of balance? Although the solutions depend to a certain degree on how the imbalance came to be, the bottom line is that you want to get your horse using his hind end, lengthening his stride length. He can not be too slow or too fast. The art of traveling straight (even on a turn) is critical as is a loosening of the body, so that the tension may dissipate.

Section 3: The Specifics

Eight Legs Plus Two

Eight legs plus two
Ambling along through the tree tunnel
With places to go but

Looking around
Smelling the breeze
Reaching for the drive-through grass nibble
Contentedly heading home.

Eight legs plus two
One strolling in between
Flanked by muscled ripples under gleaming coats
Bounding energy and strength
Gracefully contained in calm comfort.

10 legs heading home.

13 Interpreting The Half-Halt

We call it the half-halt in the english disciplines, or it is also called the "check" in western riding (I will use "half-halt" in this article to mean both terms). In some ways, the terms are awkward misnomers. We don't really want a *half of a halt*, although many people characterize it as such. What we really mean by the term is that we want the horse to create or maintain the balance needed to negotiate the next movement.

It is said that the half-halt has different meanings to different people. Certainly, if you ask different instructors to explain how to do a half-halt, you are likely to get several answers that may or may not have much in common.

We all agree on the fact that a half-halt is intended to (re)balance the horse. It helps to maintain a gait, change gaits, change directions and change paces within a gait. We should place half-halts strategically through our movements, and essentially ride "half-halt to half-halt". The more half-halts we include in our ride, the easier the horse can negotiate changes of gait, weight and balance.

What the half-halt is:

- a rebalancing of the horse, promoting a rounder outline and deeper hind leg stride

- a "heads up" moment to let the horse know that a change is coming

- an opportunity to maintain an open communication line with the horse: "Are you still with me?"

What a half-halt is not:

- a pull by the hand that affects the horse's mouth

- a shove forward by the seat and legs that causes the horse to become heavier on the forehand

The aids for the half-halt usually transpire almost invisibly between the horse and the rider. In general, the *results* of the half-halt are apparent to the onlooker.

Developing your half-halt

Learning to half-halt is one of the skills in horseback riding that will take years to develop. Just when you think you have the hang of it, you will find yet another "level" of understanding that will challenge you to progress to a deeper and more refined aid.

First steps

As they say, some kind of half-halt is better than no half-halt. Very likely, your first half-halts are going to be through your hands and not much through your other aids. You will enjoy the feel of your new skill because your horse will probably slow his feet down and shift some weight backward.

He will probably lighten on the bit and regulate his strides.

But beware: what you are feeling at this stage is not a true half-halt, but more of an extinguishing of energy. Any aid that includes a pull backward with the hands will result in a disengagement of the hocks. So even if the horse feels lighter and slower, what you are really feeling is the stoppage of energy. The horse might also hollow his back and raise his head carriage. This change of frame should be your first clue that the aids are not as effective as they could be.

Apply the half-halt as the inside hind leg strides forward. Lighten through the seat, then release forward.

Gaining a better understanding

The next stage is when you will begin to realize that the half-halt is a whole-body endeavor. The hands become less of an aiding influence, and your seat and legs begin to take on a more prominent role. At this point, you will have adequate body control and balance to be able to use your legs to ask the horse to lift his rib cage. The lightening of your seat will encourage the horse to step deeper with the hind legs, and the result will enable you to physically rebalance his entire body.

The outward picture will look like the horse has tilted his hind end and lifted through the back. The body will be rounder and the strides bigger. Often, the horse will snort or breathe audibly, indicating the strength he is putting into carrying your weight more correctly.

If you can negotiate several half-halts within a series of movements, your horse will be better able to "dance" through the requests, remaining light, balanced and round in the outline through all the changes of direction or gait.

If you feel a floating sensation, noticing that the horse's foot falls sound lighter and the gaits are becoming more flowing and easier to ride, you know you are on the right track!

The "forward" half-halt

At some point, you will progress even beyond your finest achievements to realize that the half-halt is actually a forward movement. You will relinquish the need for the hand aids (other than to support your driving aids) in preference for the surge of energy coming from the hind end thanks to your seat, weight and leg aids. You will discover the true meaning of balance through your seat and relish in the bounce, enthusiasm and sheer power the horse will offer to you, movement to movement.

Onlookers will be able to recognize the result of the half-halts because the horse will appear to flow effortlessly from one movement to the next, seemingly reading your mind, the two of you floating as one. Some may accuse you of doing nothing. Your horse will move with enthusiasm, showing off flip-floppy ears and gleaming muscles that roll under the skin like jello.

Most importantly, when your horse approves of your riding skills, and seems to connect with you even more after you get off, you will have all the reward you need!

14 How to Ride the Stumble Out of Your Horse

Do you have a horse that seems to regularly trip or stumble, either in the front or hind end? The footing is good. The path is clear. There were no sudden changes to your direction.

The horse is sound and you know the tack fits well. His feet are trimmed. Your vet has given the horse a clean bill of health and there are no other underlying physical issues that you are aware of.

Yet your horse stumbles here, trips there, and as time goes by, you learn to just quietly ignore it. After all, the horse is trying his best and there's nothing you can do, right?

WRONG!

If you listen carefully, you might even discover that you are more a part of the equation than you give yourself credit for. It might be something you are doing. Or it might be something you are NOT doing!

Be an active rider so you can help your horse through these moments. Rather than just accepting what you're getting, be a participant in the ride. Your strong problem-solving skills are just the ticket to helping your horse develop better balance during riding.

Riding Reasons for Stumbling

The root problem might be one, or a combination, of these ideas.

Horse is heavy on the forehand.

We know the tell-tale signs for that. The horse is heavy on the bit. The front leg strides are bigger than the hind leg strides. The horse might even feel like he is on a downward slope, leaning in to the ground rather than up away from it.

Horse's outline is too long and low.

This might come hand-in-hand with #1. Often, we feel we are being "nicer" to let a horse stretch his neck up and/or down, because we are taught that a softer, lighter contact is kind.

What we aren't always told is that the horse might have to brace his back and tense his muscles to hold this position, especially in order to deal with the weight of a rider in the saddle.

Add to the "strung-out" outline - a hind end that is no longer able to support the weight (because the hind legs have stretched beyond the horse's croup, thereby not allowing for any weight carriage) - and there you have it folks - the stumble!

A little shoulder-fore can help to straighten the horse so the shoulders move in line with the hips, thereby improving the horse's overall balance.

Horse speeds up faster and faster in the same gait.

A horse that tends to move his legs faster and faster when you ask for more impulsion or a gait change is a good candidate for a stumble.

Again, his weight (and yours) falls forward and the front legs have to carry the majority of the impact.

Horse has little engagement.

The opposite can also be true. The horse that "sucks back" is bracing with his front end, effectively pushing backward in the movement so that he doesn't progress forward in space.

His hind legs take short strides and the balance is leaning "downhill" to the forehand. This active tension can be a cause for stumbling.

Horse needs extra help on one side.

A horse with a weak side (for example, a weak left stifle) could have trouble bringing that hind leg up with the same amount of strength and fluidity as the other hind. After the true source of the problem is identified and addressed (i.e. call a veterinarian), you can support that side with more active riding aimed at building up the muscles around the joint.

Horse is overly crooked.

Some horses are particularly stiff to one side. This might be influenced by a natural cause (born that way), or from previous incorrect riding. In either case, much attention needs to be given to at least straightening the horse (even if it is too difficult to get a true bend) while he is moving. The rider should also assess her own crookedness and work to correct her hip and shoulder alignment as well as the horse's.

You shift your weight to the horse's forehand.

Riders often lean forward in movement. As bi-peds, it is what we are naturally programmed to do. However, "listen" carefully to your horse when he stumbles. If he tends to trip when you lean forward, you know the reason why! In this case, you will need to hold your weight back, even if you want to ride in two-point or go over a jump. You can hold your weight and change your posture - just be aware!

IN THE RING

5 Steps to Prevent Stumbling

1. Leg on for impulsion.

Even the fast-footed horse is disengaged and needs to bring his hind end underneath him. So put your legs on and be ready for more movement!

2. Commit your body to the energy surge.

The horse *should* lurch forward a bit. This is good. Go with him. Be sure you don't stop the forward inclination by pulling back on the bit.

3. Straighten the horse (if needed).

Use the energy surge to straighten the horse, left or right as needed. Just guide the energy into straightness, don't stifle it. Use any form of gymnastic exercise such as shoulder-fore or shoulder-in to line up the shoulders with the hips.

4. Half-halt.

This is key. Without the half-halt immediately after the energy surge, you essentially tell the horse to run away. You don't want your horse to flee your aids, so within a moment after your legs and straightness, you half-halt should come on (brace your seat, back, arms momentarily).

5. Then release.

Remember that a release is not the same thing as a drop.

However, there must be a following of the aids that occurs immediately after the half-halt brace so that the horse is allowed to send the energy forward and through the body.

The idea is to re-balance that energy surge to the hind end rather than let it run out the front end. Constantly work on that re-balance - you may need to do the whole thing three, four, five times in a row, in rhythm with the horse's strides, to help the horse understand he needs to shift his weight backward.

You might also discover that the horse needs this rebalancing a lot more frequently than you imagined. For example, you might need to half-halt before a corner, after a corner, as well as before and after the next corner.

You might need to rebalance before a transition and immediately after achieving the new gait. Riders are often surprised when they first realize how often half-halts might need to be applied to maintain true balance.

Stick to the exercise. Repeat many times and do not give up. Try it again for several sessions in a row, always rewarding even the smallest effort in the right direction. Avoid getting frustrated but keep working on rebalancing at key moments.

Eventually, your horse should learn to respond smoothly and easily. This might be very difficult for a horse that is not used to working from the hind end. But it is essential, first, to prevent the stumble, and second, to keep the horse sound long-term. Good luck!

15 How to Halt Without Using the Reins

A gently closed fist with a light contact is all that is needed when you halt from your seat.

Does your horse get offended when you pull on the reins to stop? Does he pin his ears, shake his head or keep going? Maybe he's trying to tell you something: stop pulling on the reins! There is a way to get your horse to stop without pulling on the reins.

But first, you both have to be "in sync" together, working in tandem instead of against each other.

If you haven't done this before, it may take a few tries to convince your horse that you want to work with him. Horses that are regularly pulled on seem to accept that the pressure has to be there before they should respond. They might learn to lean on the bit, pulling against you while you pull backward, hoping for the legs to stop.

Some horses are generous and eventually slow their feet, stop/starting until finally, all four legs come to a halt. Other horses might not be quite as forgiving and just keep going until you have to put more and more pressure on the mouth.

Eventually, one of you wins but it's never pretty!

We all dream of finding the halt that looks like we are in complete harmony with our horse. You know - the one that feels like the horse's legs are your legs, and your mind is so coordinated with the horse that it looks like you are reading each other's thoughts.

It does happen. The secret: ride from your seat.

I'm perfectly aware of the fact that we've talked about the seat many times already, but there is no other answer. Everything in horseback riding begins and ends with the seat.

Developing an effective seat is the single most important skill you can develop in horseback riding. The instructions below might sound quite complicated. Initially, developing the timing and coordination of aids should be!

Learning correct aids should be a lifelong quest for most of us, and if we have old, ingrained habits (like pulling on the reins), these changes may take even longer. In the long run, you won't have to think anything through and the aids will happen together on their own.

Set-up for a Correct Halt

1. Contact

Prepare several strides ahead of the intended location. Your reins should be a good length - not too long and not too short. There should be a steady enough contact on the bit to be able to communicate very subtle changes of pressure.

2. Begin a series of half-halts.

The half-halts start at the seat. In rhythm with the horse's movement, resist with your lower back. Be sure to resist in rhythm. In other words, your lower back and seat will feel something like this: *resist... flow... resist... flow... resist... flow.*

2a. Use your legs.

During each flow moment, squeeze lightly with your calves. This helps the horse engage his hind end deeper underneath the body in preparation with the halt.

2b. Use the hands.

During each *resist* moment, squeeze the reins with your hands. You might squeeze both reins or just one rein (the outside rein being the usual rein) but in any case, do your best to use the hands after the leg aids. The rein pressure should occur in tandem with the resisting seat aid.

3. When you are ready for the halt, simply stop your seat.

Maintain contact with your legs and reins, but stop the activity. *Don't keep pulling on the reins.* If the horse is truly with you, his legs will stop lightly and in balance.

Horses that have been trained to respond to the half-halt will sigh in relief when you lighten up on your aids and use your seat in the halt. You might be surprised at how easily the legs will stop if you can improve your timing and releases.

Horses that have always been pulled on might not respond at all. They might be expecting to be hauled backward, thrown to the forehand, and dragged to a stop. If this is the case, be patient. If you haven't done this before, it may take a few tries to convince your horse that you want to work with him.

You might have to bridge the learning gap by applying the half-halts several times, stopping your seat and then pulling to stop. In the end though, the pull should disappear completely from your vocabulary (exception: in an emergency stop).

16 Don't Mistake the Halt For A Stop

Don't do it! Don't mistake the halt for a stop.

They are two entirely different maneuvers.

Avoid using the terms 'halt' and 'stop' interchangeably. They are completely distinct. The stop is as it says - a complete stop. Done. Over with, done that. Finished. Use the stop at the end of your ride, just before you get off.

The halt is far removed from the stop. It is a movement, and as such, it is just as engaged, energy-bound, and balanced as any other movement the horse can do. Think of it as a canter - without the legs moving, or the progression through space. Picture a car stopped at the red light. The engine is on and the moment of departure is at hand. Your horse should be ready and prepared to proceed to any movement you ask directly out of the halt.

Develop a rhythm, and maintain the momentum.

The halt has a rhythm similar to the rest of the movements. It also has momentum. The horse's hind legs go underneath the body and are prepared and waiting to step into the next movement at a moment's notice.

Don't break the momentum - even when you go to halt.

If you 'stop' instead of halt, the momentum is lost and the horse loses balance, strength and precision. The body becomes flat. The legs feel like they are 'stuck in the mud.' It is virtually impossible to do anything other than stagger out of the stop. The horse seems surprised if you ask for something after the stop.

Because the secret is that the halt is still a *movement*.

In classical dressage, the halt is considered a movement. By definition, the halt is a "suspension of progress, especially a temporary one." It is a pause, but it is just that. Keep the horse round - similar to a nice trot - and just stop the forward progression through space.

It is NOT a stop-moving-your-feet-and-throw-it-all-away feeling.

It is more of a wait-wait-wait-and-now-GO feeling.

You NEED your legs going into the stop!

The horse should round its back and reach *further* underneath the body with the hind legs - all of this happens before the halt. Use your legs to lift the back before the horse halts. Keep the horse straight and half-halt into the movement. Avoid using your hands to pull on the horse's mouth. Instead, halt from your seat. THEN, halt from the hind end. The front end remains balanced and light. The back is round, the contact is consistent. The legs will stop square if the approach into the halt is energetic, forward and balanced.

Be ready to gracefully step out of the pause at a moment's notice - to walk, trot or canter.

P.S. One last thought.

The "test" for the halt: the horse is round, reaching for the bit, and SQUARE with all four legs. Then you know you are on the right track!

IN THE RING

One way you can develop an energetic halt is to trot to the halt.

Start with a good forward-moving trot.

Increase energy a few strides before the halt, using a series of half-halts in tandem with the surge of energy.

You will need to activate your leg aids as well as the seat to encourage more activity. Think of it as a revving up of the engine just before you hit the breaks.

Then, stop everything.

Avoid pulling backward on the reins. It is essential for the energy that you built up to have a place to go - over the horse's top line and "through" in a way that doesn't stifle the horse's forward enthusiasm.

However, keep using half-halts as necessary to help keep the horse balanced into the new "gait."

At first, the horse may take two to three steps in walk before coming to a full halt. Accept this at the beginning stages but as the horse improves, work toward a trot to halt transition. The strong trot sets up an active halt from the hind end.

If you feel your horse's hind end tilt under into the halt, you know you are developing a strong and secure halt. If your horse's legs are square underneath him, you know you are achieving your goal.

If the horse can move out of the halt with commitment and expression at a moment's notice, you know that you have found the halt that isn't really a halt but is more of a movement!

17 Do A "Forward" Back-Up

How do you get a horse to back up lightly, energetically and rhythmically?

Do it "forward!"

It sounds like an oxymoron, but it's the truth. You MUST make the back-up into a forward movement. That is the only way the horse can move his legs efficiently and diagonally.

The back-up is a very important part of the correct training of the horse. It is the beginning of teaching the horse to tilt his hind end and carry more weight on his haunches. It is the preparatory step for a good walk-canter departure and for many of the upper-level movements. But first, you must teach the horse to step backward without creating tension and sticky steps.

How NOT to back up

You will often see people pulling on their horse's mouth and kicking. The horse might open his mouth, tighten and raise the neck, and step back stiff-legged like his legs are stuck in quicksand.

The first thing to keep in mind is to NEVER pull backward on the reins (not for any other movements either, but especially not for the back-up).

4 steps to a good back-up

1. Shorten the reins so you have contact. How much contact depends on the level of understanding of your horse. If this is a new movement, you might need more contact. If the horse is far enough along, you could get away with a "whisper" of a contact! This is what we are all aiming for. But in the interest of being clear with our aids, we might need to use more pressure at first so there is no guess work for the horse.

However, please note that contact does not mean a pull-back. Although you make the reins short enough to put some pressure on the horse's mouth, the reins are not actively moving backward toward your body.

2. Start with a gentle squeeze of your legs. Do not kick unless you absolutely have to. If the horse gives no response, you might need to kick. Otherwise, a squeeze should activate the hind legs enough to *almost* take a step forward.

3. As the horse takes that forward step, he leans into the pressure of the contact and realizes that he cannot step ahead. The legs then begin the backward movement. At the same time, lighten your seat slightly to the front of the saddle. The

weight shift should be so small that it is not visible - only the horse and you know that you shifted your seat. This frees up the back under the saddle so that the horse can lift his hind legs and tilt the haunches.

4. Once the backward motion has started, lighten the contact (don't throw it all away) in order to give the horse a release. Stay light in the seat while the horse takes the steps. You stop the backward motion by sitting back into a normal seat. Your seat, followed by light leg aids, then drive your horse forward into the same light contact. The difference is that this time, you walk forward.

Always walk forward out of a back-up. You want to regularly instill a "forward attitude" into the horse, especially after a back-up.

Possible corrections

Beginning horses often resist taking the backward steps as the shift of weight back is unusual for horses to do on their own. Just be patient through the initial stages and insist that the horse moves his legs backward before you stop your aids.

Wait through the confusion of the horse even if he throws his head sideways or up. The legs might drag backwards or you might get one step, then another, then a stop. It doesn't matter; just keep at it until you think he has understood.

It might take several sessions before the horse lightens and begins to understand what you are asking for. Keep the energy level up, look for diagonal pairs of legs moving together, and work toward keeping a soft neck and poll through the movement. Find the balance between trying again and knowing when it is time to stop.

He will get better with time.

IN THE RING

From the walk, develop a halt. Remember that the energy in the halt will need to be maintained, and is usually proportional to the energy in the walk before the halt. Wait for a few seconds after achieving the halt.

Take up any loose reins, put your legs on and lighten your seat (just a feeling - don't actually lean forward). Use your voice and think, "back."

Wait for the horse to take his first steps backward. Reward for any attempt. He should feel like he was going to take a step forward but your hands didn't allow the energy through, so he "bounced" off the bit and proceeded to step backward.

As he takes his first few steps back, your reins soften to allow for a release of the bit *through* the movement. Ideally, you want the horse to back up from your leg and seat aids, not your hands. So always release as he moves, even if that means that he ends up stopping. Over time, he will learn to keep moving until your seat and legs stop asking for movement.

Develop the back-up by asking for more steps over time. Then ask for faster steps to get the diagonal movement of the legs.

Section 4: The Solutions

18 Drawing A Circle (In Sand)

One of the most fundamental exercises in most riding disciplines is the circle.

If you are a newcomer to horseback riding, you will likely meet the circle early on in your career, as it is beneficial in many ways to both the horse and the rider. As a veteran rider, you are likely all-too-familiar with the smooth curves and rounding suppleness that results in your horse after a series of various sized circles.

But what really is a circle? What does it look like when completed correctly and what figures can be classified as NOT circles?

Moving straight but not really...

It is true that riding round and round the ring on the fence line (or track or rail) is one of the easiest things you can be doing on horseback. The second easiest thing to do (not necessarily well) is to ride a line from end to end of the ring. Just point the horse's nose and hang on!

What is perhaps less well known is that moving along a *straight* line is in fact one of the most difficult movements a horse has to learn. Although many people assume that a straight line is an easily completed "figure", moving straight *correctly* is rarely achieved. Watch carefully and you will notice the horse's hind end pointing toward the inside of the ring, or the hind footprints not falling over the front footprints.

Enter the circle!

Just like people, horses have a preferred side and tend to want to bear more weight to that side. They are just as uneven as we are. Becoming more ambidextrous is as long a process for them as it is for us to learn to use both sides of our bodies. And perhaps ironically, one of the most effective ways to develop better straight lines is to ride a circle.

Why should you even bother with a circle?

The primary intention of riding a circle is to help your horse loosen in the muscles and develop suppleness in his movement. It evens out the horse's ability to bear weight in the hind end, and stretches both sides of the horse.

If you feel the horse stiffening on a long line, change course and head into a circle.

If you find your horse is distracted or spooking at something outside the arena, the circle is a tried-and-true method to bring his attention back to the (boring) center of the ring.

If you find your horse being uneven in his striding, or leaning in/drifting out, or moving in an otherwise "crooked" manner, then the circle is just right to help him straighten out through his body.

If your horse is a runner and speeds up with increasing tension, put him on a circle and allow him to slow down thanks to the increased weight bearing of the inside hind leg. Using a circle makes it easy for the horse to want to naturally slow his rhythm. You do not have to use as much rein pressure just because the circle will enable the horse to balance better on his own.

What does a circle look like?

A correctly ridden circle is even and round. I know - that must sound obvious! However, unless you have spent hours on perfecting the circle, you will agree with me that maintaining shape and ease of movement is easier said than done.

Regardless of where you position the circle in the arena, it should be evenly spaced and round. You must end the circle where you began it, and the diameters should be even - if it is a 20 meter circle, there should be twenty meters from end to end regardless of where you are currently positioned.

The "NOT" Circle

The "NOT circle" isn't quite nearly as useful as the "NOT Canter"!

There are many variations of the not circle - and all of them are not circles!

A - This circle is one of the most common not circles mainly because of its pseudo-roundness. While you are riding the figure, you are quite sure that you have completed a round figure.

The NOT Circle!

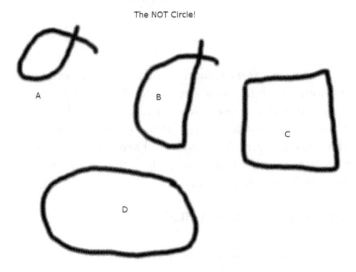

That is, until you either look at the footprints in the sand or listen to your instructor's feedback! This circle does not start nor end at the same place and isn't quite evenly round. The horse probably fell in to the middle shortly after the beginning of the circle.

B - This is another common not circle because it is so easy to lose sight of the second half of the circle. Riders often start with good intentions (staying round through the first two quadrants of the circle), and through various inaccuracies - maybe the horse falls in to the middle, or the rider pulls on the inside rein too strongly - the circle ends in an abrupt straight line.

C - Here is another common error - the circle that follows the rail. In the end, you discover that you made a rectangle that basically left one rail and headed straight to another. This figure completely negates the purpose of the circle, as the horse doesn't bend through the body. On the other hand, a well-ridden square - OFF the rail - is an extremely beneficial exercise although not at all what we are discussing here.

D - Despite the fact that this final not circle is ever so close to being true, it is not even through the quadrants and therefore ends up becoming more of an oval than a circle. Once again, the horse can avoid bending on the long sides and likely uses the rail as a guideline on where to go.

IN THE RING

Get out in the ring and be the rider who practices circles to perfection. Work on developing your horse's suppleness and bend, and help him learn to carry more weight on his inside hind leg. Learn the circle aids well and soon enough, "drawing" round, even circles in the sand will become (almost) second nature!

Starting on the rail to the right, pick two or four points to leave the rail for a fairly large (20m) circle. Pick specific points - perhaps at A and C - and complete circles precisely at those letters. For an overly energetic horse, do four circles each time around the ring - at A, E, C and B.

You might choose to keep all the circles the same size. Or you might want to alternate: large-small-large-small. Make sure you go both ways and practice both sides of the horse.

For added challenge, change gaits for specific circles., or change directions. Do a figure eight and then go back to the rail and resume the circles at each letter.

Use your imagination to add variety in size, gait and direction and soon enough, you will begin to connect like dancing partners!

19 Secrets of A Great Turn

If you "listen" carefully, can you feel your horse's subtle weight shifts when you begin a turn? Can you tell if your horse uses his hind end before taking the first step in the new direction, or does he feel stiff and awkward, almost like he's leaving his legs behind the movement?

Most horses will enter a turn in the latter manner, if nothing is done to "set up" the turn in the first place.

What You Don't Want

You will know this type of turn by identifying these signs.

He will brace against the reins. You might find that he increases the pressure on your hands, gets hollow in his back, and shortens his stride length (in the hind end) as he goes into the turn.

He may throw his shoulder toward the ground. This looks and feels like the horse goes momentarily "stick-legged" - rather than flowing easily underneath you, the leg feels rigid and unmovable. Generally, he will lose steam through the turn - it feels like he is lazy and unwilling to go forward.

Finally, he will probably lift his neck and head in an effort to counteract the imbalance to the forehand. It is likely that he will continue through the turn, and the legs will take you where you want to go, but the posture and balance of the horse is compromised through the entire movement.

What You Do Want - "Stepping out" into the turn

In contrast, the well-prepared turn looks and feels very different from the above. Before beginning the turn, the horse shifts his weight, steps further under his body with his hind legs, rounds his back, and reaches for the bit.

He increases his impulsion (even if it appears like no change to the onlooker) and appears to be eagerly (not necessarily quickly) moving forward. When he begins the turn, the change of direction seems effortless and intentional. The legs just flow in rhythmical, ground-covering fashion.

And as always, the rider appears to be doing nothing!

4 Steps to a Great Turn

Step 1: Shift the horse's weight to the outside (using the inside rein and leg).

Step 2: Support the bend with the outside rein and leg.

Step 3: "Bounce" off the outside aids (inside rein should be light and used only to keep the flexion of the head in the direction of the turns).

Step 4: Inside front leg reaches inward to the first turn step, followed lightly by the body.

Step 1 and 2: These occur on the straight line before heading into the turn. This is also the moment of engagement - when the horse reaches further underneath the body, lifts the back, rounds and reaches for contact. The weight shifts to the outside just enough to allow the inside of the horse to free up to step into the turn. Once Step 2 is complete, the horse is prepared with a nice light bend, ready to take the first turn step.

Step 3: The "bounce" is the result of your outside aids becoming active. It feels like first you embrace the horse as he fills your outside rein and leg, and then you become active and gently urge him to step away from it all. Through this step, you maintain an inside flexion first with your inside leg and then with your inside rein.

The perfect Step 3 feels like you have a fluttering contact with your inside rein, and the horse is lightly wrapped around your inside leg but pleasantly swelled to the outside. Your own body is exactly in balance with the horse - your hips and shoulders open into the turn in parallel with your horse's shoulders.

Step 4: The horse is now taking his first step into the turn. It is as if you set it all up, and now you are setting the horse free! Here, you just follow - with your seat, hands and balance.

You now have a choice - take another step into the turn, or come out of the turn.

Don't be in a rush!

In general, it may take several strides to achieve Steps 1 to 3. Your horse may continue to brace/throw his head/drop the shoulder, maybe even worse than before you tried to set him up. Learn to wait through the upheaval. Keep your aids on calmly but insistently and wait for the moment that you can reward him - even for a small change in the right direction.

Try this at the walk, then trot and canter. Your horse should always enter a turn the same way - shift out to turn in.

One last thought: do not rush the turn, for the turn itself is not the end goal. The goal of this (and any) movement is to help your horse achieve balance within the movement. The movement itself is a breeze after that!

<u>IN THE RING</u>

Try using a corner of the arena to set up a successful turn. Ride into the corner with a mild bend to the inside. As you go through the corner, shift out.

Once the shift is completed, and the horse is securely on the outside leg and rein aids, allow the horse to take the first inside step that will initiate the turn. At first, accept just one or two turn steps.

Later, expect more steps in a row. Finally, move the horse out of the corner and expect the same results.

The idea is to replace the support of the rail with your outside aids. The point to stepping out is to develop your outside leg and rein aids so they can act as "the wall" - without having a physical wall to do it for you.

Turn position: rider's inside leg at the girth, outside leg behind the girth, outside rein on the neck and soft inside rein (not visible).

Eventually, shifting out for balance will become second nature for both you and the horse and it will become a part of every turn!

20 Why You Should Ride the Left Side of the Horse

When you ride your horse, do you notice if your horse is stiff to one side? Like people, most horses have a dominant and non-dominant side. Funny enough, the side that the horse feels stiffest on is his stronger side

For the purpose of examples below, we will assume our horse is stiff going to the left.

Feel the Different Sides

People often refer to them as the stiff side and the hollow side. The stiff side feels just like the description - there is more tension in the body. The horse's jaw and poll is tighter and more resistant. The body might feel like one giant slab of plywood!

The horse tends to lean into the stiffer side, falling into a circle or making tight and abrupt turns. You might think that the horse disregards the aids more to the stiff side.

On the other hand, the hollow side often feels like there is no resistance. You have to work to maintain contact on the hollow side because the horse has a tendency to give in to any pressure so deeply that there is no weight on your reins or legs.

When moving in the direction of the hollow side, the horse will want to drift to the outside, often bent (or over bent) in the direction of movement.

Three Common Causes of Stiffness

1. Left or right handed?

It might seem counter-intuitive to think that the right-handed horse is stiffer to the left side. But the right-handed horse is stronger in the right hind leg. Therefore, the horse will be stronger moving to the left (ie when the right hind is working on the outside of the body). When moving to the left direction, he can brace easier, support our weight easier, and balance better. He will also usually have an easier time picking up the left lead.

If the horse is right-dominant, he will generally be stronger moving to the left and therefore have an easier time resisting your aids! Surprisingly, although the tension is there, most movements will feel stronger and more coordinated going left.

2. Uneven muscle development?

Another cause of stiffness may be due to contracted muscling on one side of the body. The horse that is stiff to the left will be contracted in the muscles of the right side of the body. However, the muscles on his left side will be over stretched. That is why he will want to move overbent to the right. It is simply easier for the horse.

3. How about the rider?

Let's not forget the rider in the equation. Some horses travel stiffly to one side because their <u>rider</u> is contracted to one side. Do you collapse easily on your left side? Many right-handed people do. Many of us pull back with our left hand and push our right side forward. Needless to say, our one-sided-ness often starts at the seat. If your seat is lopsided to the left, you will invariably and unknowingly be affecting your horse's ability to move correctly.

Regardless of the reason for the stiffness, all stiffness is demonstrated through crookedness.

Obsess over straightness.

Sometimes, it's ok to be a little obsessive. You can never overdo straightening your horse. Like so many other components of riding, such as perfecting an effective seat or learning a true half-halt, developing straightness in your horse will take years to accomplish. Each time you think you are on the right track, you will discover yet another "problem" that needs to be mastered in order to encourage true ambidextrous movement.

Work the stiff side in BOTH directions.

Most of us go along with the status quo, opting to move with the horse rather than working against him - even if it means that working against him might change his way of going for the better. Effective riding means that we must always strive to improve his weight carriage and balance.

117

Keep the left side of the horse straight while preparing to travel right.

If the horse is moving to the right, we work the right side of the horse. We know we should bend into the direction of movement, and therefore, we apply our inside aids and ask for the bend to the right.

What we may not realize right away is that due to uneven muscle development, the horse is already bent to the right.

In order to help straighten the horse (to elongate the muscles on the right side, and help the horse bear more weight on the left hind leg), we need to work on the left side going right. In other words, we need to apply our left aids to help keep the horse straight when he wants to hollow to the right. This will also help us maintain better contact with our inside aids.

When you have a horse that is stiff on *one* side, ride that side in both directions.

Going right.

Explore with putting more weight into your left seat bone. Ask for a mild left bend (which will only result in straightness) starting from your seat.

Keep a straighter and possibly stronger left rein. Keep a more supportive left leg on the horse - either behind the girth to prevent the hind end from drifting out, or at the girth to keep a straighter rib cage. Maintain contact with your right rein - even if your horse wants to bend in so deeply that he can completely eliminate the contact.

Try to keep your horse's hind legs tracking directly into the front legs. This might require a mild haunches-in so that the hips are in line with the shoulders.

It might take a very long while for your horse (and you) to develop the even muscling and strength that is required to be truly ambidextrous. However, if you address stiffness at every turn (pun intended!), you will be surprised at how much your horse can improve!

IN THE RING

Ride your horse in both directions, taking note of the stiff and hollow sides. Now, regardless of which direction you go, put extra effort into keeping the neck and body straight.

Try using aids on the same side going in both directions. If your horse tracks his hind footprints into his front footprints, you are on the right track.

If he begins to have an easier time bending in the direction of the turn, you are doing well.

Keep at it. Be willing to work more consistently on the side that needs extra attention. Over time, you will discover that your horse begins to track straighter and have an easier time bending left and right. Maybe your rein contact becomes more even on the left and right reins and the horse has less difficulty negotiating turns and circles.

As your horse improves, don't forget about your own flexibility and ambidextrousness! Surely, if you expect your horse to work freely on both sides, you should do the same!

21 What To Do When a Half-Halt Just Won't Do

It has probably happened to you too many times to mention. Coming to a turn, you asked for a half-halt.

Preparing for a transition, you wanted a soft rebalancing before the new gait.

Half-way around the circle, you half-halted in order to prevent your horse from leaning in or out.

You felt your horse stiffen and you used a half-halt to ask him to loosen once again.

Maybe all you wanted to do was get your horse's attention before the next transition.

...and NOTHING HAPPENED!

Your horse did not understand.

He tensed his head and neck and went against your half-halt.

He hollowed his back and ran faster and faster (or conversely, shuffled along slower and slower).

Maybe he flat out ignored you!

In the end, it doesn't really matter why the half-halt did not "go through". There could be a thousand and one reasons why! The fact is, it did not work.

What Not To Do

Push the horse so he gets tighter/faster/stronger and works against your aids.

Do more of the same and expect different results.

Get offended by his personal vendetta against you!

Give up.

Looking Closer

Balance does not happen magically on its own. When you watch a gorgeous horse and rider combination apparently floating along weightlessly, reading each other's minds, recognize that they are continually balancing and rebalancing gait to gait, stride to stride and moment to moment.

The idea is to help the horse keep his weight on the hind end (rather than fall to the forehand) before, during and after transitions. Because a half-halt is not a slowing down aid, the horse should ideally keep up his energy and impulsion while simultaneously shifting his balance off his forehand.

When a horse has difficulty rebalancing in movement (for whatever reason), he simply can't help you in that moment. So you have to find another way to explain that he should take his weight to the hind end.

What To Do

I like to think of it as a "full" half-halt. Not as in a full halt. Far from it.

Instead of trying the half-halt over and over, just follow through until the horse does a full transition down from the gait you were at. If you were in canter, go to trot. If you were in trot, go to walk. If you were already in walk, go to an under-power walk (not halt, obviously).

Wait at the slower gait until you get what you want. Perhaps you needed a shoulder out of the way. Maybe you wanted a rounder body outline. Maybe you were asking for the hind legs to reach deeper underneath the body.

In all those cases, do a full downward transition, work at the more controlled (= balanced) gait, get what you wanted, and then go right back to what you were doing.

Don't Forget!

The one downfall to this technique is that many riders fall into the "slower is better" rut. Keep in mind that you are not exactly trying to slow the horse down. You do not want to lose the energy or impulsion you already have.

Rather, you are helping him to balance better before you increase the difficulty at a higher gait. One thing you want to avoid is to do a downward transition and stay there. As soon as you feel the horse has balanced and responded to your aid, go back to your original task.

Immediately switch back to canter, if that was the gait you were working at. Then do the same lesson you were doing, ask with a half-halt, and see what happens.

Your horse might respond quite nicely. You will say "yes" and go to the next thing.

Your horse might not respond at all. In this case, you should do another "full half-halt". You might need to do it a few times in a row until your horse is better able to work from his haunches.

One time, after several repetitions of "full half-halt", try the half-halt again. It just might happen that your horse has an easier time sitting down and balancing to the hind end.

If you have a softer, more responsive horse, you know you are on the right track.

If your horse feels more supple and loose over the topline, you know you are getting closer.

If your horse catapults you out of your tack with heartfelt snorts, you know you've got the ticket! :)

22 Riding Straight Through the Turn

Do you have trouble with your turns? Does your horse flatten out in the corners, falling in rather than going deep into the turn? Maybe your horse "pops" a shoulder to the inside or outside?

On a circle, do you find yourself drifting out at times, falling in to the middle of the circle at other times or even doing both from stride to stride? If so, then it is important to focus on straightening your horse through the turns.

Go straight in a turn

Although it sounds like an oxymoron, traveling straight through a turn is essential in maintaining the balance of the horse.

Moving straight allows the hind end to step underneath the horse and bear the weight correctly, rather than falling heavily to the front legs.

A straight-moving horse negotiates a turn effortlessly. He can keep his round outline and move boldly into the next strides simply because he is able to use his body in an efficient way.

There are many ways to work on straightening, including stepping out as well as shoulder-in and haunches in. The technique depends on the reason behind the crookedness.

In this chapter, we will focus on one aid to help the shoulders stay centered so that the horse's stride can reach forward and through the body rather than fall to the inside or outside.

Keep in mind that this is just one small aspect of the whole aiding process - but a missing rein aid could be just the part that is permitting the lack of straightness.

Keeping the shoulders in the body

1. Lower your hand to wither height.

2. Keep the contact short enough so the horse feels your aid, but not so short that it interferes with the horse's movement.

3. Steady the rein momentarily as the horse begins to fall to the inside or outside. Use a direct rein pressure (rather than indirect).

DO NOT PULL BACKWARD!

4. Use the rein aid to block the shoulder that wants to pop in or out.

5. Release the rein aid as soon as the horse's shoulder is stepping forward and through the body.

The trick is to redirect the energy

The idea is to take the same energy that the horse is going to use to step sideways, and redirect it forward and straight. You can think of it as a "bounce" - as in, bounce the shoulder away from the rein toward the center of the body.

As always, the key is in the release of the rein. Remember that this is a correction. As with all corrections, you only use it during the moment that it is needed, and no longer.

"Bouncing" the horse off the inside rein.

If the rein is held too long, the corresponding hind leg may be blocked from reaching underneath the body, and the effect will be directly counterproductive to what you are trying to achieve. So you have to feel for the moment, apply the aid, and then release it as soon as possible in order to allow the free movement forward.

You can use this rein aid on the inside rein or the outside rein, depending on what is happening with the movement. You can even use them consecutively. If the horse is falling in, use the inside shoulder block, and before the horse falls through the outside shoulder (a common reaction), apply the outside shoulder block.

Theoretically, the outside rein should be the rein that provides stability for the horse anyway, so it should be active through the correction.

So there we have it! In real time, this aid takes less than a second and should be used in conjunction with the usual seat and leg aids. As with most corrections, be sure to encourage impulsion at the end of the correction, since without energy forward, there is no point to anything! Your horse will let you know that you are on the right track if he seems to move freer, swings through the body better (releases tension), rounds and/or gives you a hearty snort!

23 Use the Canter-Trot to Engage the Hind End

The word "engagement" is second to none when it comes to horseback riding. All the disciplines ask for hind end engagement, from western performance to dressage to jumping to endurance riding - there is no other way to move than from the hind end!

We know why we want engagement: if we can get the horse moving "from the hind end," the horse can stay sound even while ridden into old age. With more weight shifted to the hind end, there is less dragging on the forehand. There is better weight bearing over the back, and the lighter footfalls save the joints and tendons. Energy from the hind end is the prerequisite for horse riding heaven and we all know that!

However, we might not be quite as accomplished when it really comes down to figuring out how we can develop hind end engagement. Many riders think that kicking the horse along and making the legs move faster is the ticket to engagement - but, as discussed in the last chapter, there is nothing further from the truth!

The key to engagement is to initiate the movement from the horse's hind end, not the front end or shoulders.

So if faster isn't the answer, then what is?

We need to find out how to ask the horse to reach deeper underneath the body without throwing their weight to the forehand, and without speeding up the leg tempo.

There are many methods to teaching engagement but the "canter-trot" is relatively easy for both the horse and rider. It also accomplishes the main purpose of shifting the weight to the hind end and waking up the horse's rear engine muscles.

How to "Canter-Trot"

> Start from any gait (even a reverse)
> Canter (no more than three strides)
> Then Trot

Before you get insulted by the seemingly simple instructions above, please take note: it's not as easy as it sounds!

Possible Errors

There might be several unwanted responses you will have to redirect before you get the desired result.

1. The horse wants to canter off into the sunset.

Many horses transition into the canter but then resist breaking back into the trot. There may be many reasons why but invariably, horses have an easier time staying in the canter (and eventually getting heavier and heavier to the forehand). This is because it takes a lot of hind end work to break the momentum of the canter!

Remember that this exercise is not intended to be a canter exercise. It is a canter-TROT exercise, so the horse has to break back into the trot within one, two or three canter strides. Any longer and the hind end does not need to engage. The secret is in the transitions up and down - not in the canter gait itself.

2. The horse trots faster.

To engage the hind end, the horse *must* take a few canter strides. Just moving the legs faster into the trot is completely counterproductive to establishing hind end engagement.

If the horse just trots along faster, half-halt into a slower trot rhythm, and ask for the canter again.

Then trot.

3. The horse shows discomfort.

There might be ear pinning, tail swishing, teeth grinding, hopping... you name it. Basically, the horse is indicating either physical discomfort or mental stress.

First, ensure that there is nothing wrong with the tack, and there is nothing otherwise physically bothering the horse. If the horse is demonstrating confusion or frustration, you are likely taking him out of his comfort zone (where the comfort might indicate a typical on-the-forehand movement). A tail swish or pinned ears might indicate that you are asking him to do something that he honestly finds difficult.

In this case, be gentle, calm and patient but be firm! Many horses get used to working on a heavy forehand and initially resist bearing weight on the hind legs. If this happens to be the case, then teaching the horse hind end engagement is even more essential than you think!

Keep trying for the canter and when you get it, trot.

What happens after the canter?

After the few canter strides, break back into the trot. This trot should be very different from the trots before the canter. It should feel more active, bouncier and even *slower*. If the hind legs are truly reaching farther underneath the body, the stride might become longer and more ground covering.

At this point, you might want to enjoy the trot you have and move into further trot work from here. You might want to develop even more engagement and do a few more canter-trots in a row.

Alternately, you might want to move into a completely new movement that benefits from the deeper engagement you just achieved.

IN THE RING

The key to the canter-trot is that you are not cantering for the sake of cantering. Instead, you canter to improve the trot. The focus is still on trot development.

Therefore, from the trot, ask for a canter. As soon as possible, go back to the trot. At first, the horse might be surprised to be required to trot again (especially if you usually canter on and on). Do what you must to get that trot again.

As soon as the trot is reached, go with the energy surge that was brought on by the canter. Go with the horse - in your seat, your upper body, hands and even legs. Enjoy the longer rhythm, bounce more, sit deeper and post longer.

Keep the canter-trot always at the ready, to be used whenever the horse seems lethargic, under-power or non-reactive. Feel the horse as he straightens out, becomes more uphill, flows freer and snorts. Then, you know you are on the right track!

24 Can You Recognize the Sewing Machine Trot?

It's called a sewing-machine trot because of the up-and-down movement of the legs. We sometimes call the horse a "leg-mover" and basically mean the same thing. Essentially, the horse lacks adequate length of stride in the movement.

The legs move but the body does not go anywhere. The horse does not use his torso in the movement. Rather, he is often tight and tense through the body, and there is little swinging in the gait. Sometimes, we mistake the lack of progress as smoothness, but it really is rigidity in horse's the back and joints.

It is easy to get fooled into thinking that the sewing-machine trot is a good trot. When you are on the horse, the frenetic movement might make you think that the horse is working well. It is moving, after all!

But what is sometimes less apparent is that all the movement happens without support from the hind end.

Clues

In fact, the back is often hollow and the energy does not flow back to front. The head may be held high, the base of the neck low, and the majority of the horse's weight falls to the forehand.

One of the easiest identification factors of the sewing-machine trot is lack of "tracking up". The hind leg stride is so short that it falls one or two footprint lengths short of stepping into the front footprints.

You might also notice that the front legs take a bigger stride than the hind legs. In pictures, the hind legs appear close together underneath the hind end area, rather than drawing equal an upside-down "v" with the one made by the front legs.

What To Do

First, slow the legs down. Reduce the tempo and allow the horse to develop better balance. Let his feet catch up to his body, so he doesn't feel like is constantly running away.

Second, once you feel the tempo become more reasonable, address the hind end. Ask for more engagement by using the canter-trot or a similar exercise. Just be careful to not allow the tempo to increase again. Speed is not the intention.

Third, after you feel the burst of engagement, use a half-halt to balance the energy. Don't let it go "out the front end."

Rather, contain it and allow the energy to create a longer stride and more movement over the back.

Slow the rhythm but increase the energy level to eliminate the sewing-machine trot.

Look for a slower rhythm, but a stronger energy surge. Feel more bounce to the movement. Thanks to the increased impulsion, notice that the horse naturally wants to round more and reach better for the bit.

Through it all, avoid pulling back. Instead, keep working on half-halts, impulsion and a resulting slow(er) rhythm.

<u>IN THE RING</u>

Feel the bounce.
Get a longer stride.
Develop a slower tempo.
Post longer at the trot.
See the shoulders reach forward and long.

Hear the wind whistle past your ears (yes, even in an indoor arena).

Incorporate the tips above right into your regular riding exercises and movements. Any one will take you toward and truer trot.

Combined, they may help your horse work stronger from the hind end. Give them a try!

THEN, you know you are successfully working through the sewing machine trot.

25 The "Not-Canter"

Some horses get into an emotional (and physical) bind when it comes to canter transitions. At times, it can happen even to the best of horses - a new learning phase with higher expectations might spark either mental, emotional or even physical stress. There may be ear pinning, tail swishing, hopping, kicking out, teeth grinding - so many signs that your horse might be finding the task too difficult.

Every time you ask (with the correct aids), the horse resists. The situation becomes ugly - you have a hard enough time just sitting the bounciness, never mind getting the transition. You kick, use your voice, use the crop, rock your body over the forehand of the horse - anything to get that canter!

The horse's response can range from a mild hesitation to an outright buck or rear. Eventually, you win - the horse launches himself into a lurched, scrambling canter, running off at warp speed just to keep the three-beat gait. The strides feel awkward and unbalanced.

Many riders feel that the discomfort must be a sort of right of passage, and the horse must be driven through this awkward and unbalanced phase. Surely, the horse MUST give in one day and eventually settle into a nice calm, rhythmical canter - it only takes time and enough repetition of force.

Right?

Well, probably not.

It is true that some horses do "give in" and eventually canter more promptly - but there will always be an element of tension and lack of balance. What needs to be changed is the pattern of asking - the horse needs to be shown how to be calm and confident in the canter departure.

There are many methods to teaching a good transition but the "not canter" works easily and well if performed with gentleness and empathy. It is actually very simple - the difficult part is the waiting and patience that is required.

How to "Not Canter"

> Establish a good calm, slow, rhythmical trot.
> Apply the aids for the canter.
> Then *do not canter.*
> That's it!

Of course, your horse will react the same way he has the past hundred times. He'll pin his ears, shake his head, grind his teeth. He'll tighten his back and brace himself for a launch into the canter universe.

And you will NOT.

You will keep trotting - keep the rhythm, staying steady, slow, *calm*. Wait until he releases the tension, finishes the hops and tail swishes. Wait for the sigh of relief when he realizes that he *doesn't* have to perform on the spot.

Re-establish the trot.

Then, ask for the "not canter" again.

Keep doing this and wait for the horse to respond more calmly to your aids. He may be confused at first - why ask for something when you don't want it? But eventually, he'll see that the canter aids don't have to cause all that tension.

Celebrate!

If he happens to momentarily reach further underneath himself with his hind legs, you will celebrate. If he snorts and swings better in the trot, you will celebrate. If you discover that he takes larger trot strides, you will celebrate. Because even though these are not the canter, they are all the prerequisites to a *good* canter. They are all mini-steps in the right direction.

Then ask for another "not canter". And another. And another.

One time (probably sooner than you expect), the horse will canter. But it will be hesitant, slow stepping, breaking back to the trot. And you will celebrate that too!

Stick to the program - calm, slow, rhythmical trot. Put on the aids again: "not canter".

Wait for the next canter attempts, and once or twice, accept the canter. Do your best to follow the movement - but don't force it. Accept tentative attempts. Encourage by petting and ONE time, ask for a real canter. If there is a hint of tension, back off and "not canter" again.

Feel free to quit at any time that you feel your horse has somewhat calmed. You can always pick it up again tomorrow.

And be confident knowing that this "not" path to the canter is much faster and truer than any method that requires force. Your aim is to prove to the horse that you will always give him the benefit of the doubt, and that you are willing to wait for the "results".

Happy riding!

Note: The "not" technique can be used for any movement: the "not trot" (from a walk), the "not walk" (from a trot or canter), the "not shoulder-in", etc. It is essentially a frame of mind - can be used anywhere and any time!

**Caution: The "not canter" might not be helpful in all circumstances. If a young horse is cantering for the very first time, this would be counterproductive. Also, there may be instances where a horse might become too excited if the energy is contained too long.

Always use your best judgment in using any techniques, and seek the help of a more advanced rider/trainer if necessary. And always let the horse be your guide - you should be able to identify fairly quickly if the horse appreciates the technique.

IN THE RING

Doing the not-canter might be a bit confusing for both you and your horse at first. How can you ask for something and then not go through with it? Sounds extremely counter-intuitive, especially when we are routinely taught to make sure we get what we asked for before moving on.

But put that thought aside and give it a good try. You will start to realize, as you try this technique, that for whatever reason, your horse will start to settle down and release the tension that has been plaguing him till now. He might give a heartfelt snort, slow his rhythm, soften his topline, and generally lose the tightness and bracing, even though he is still only trotting.

This release through the muscles is precisely what you are looking for - even if there is no canter yet.

You might want to go to something else for a while, especially if you were able to soften the horse and get him to be more on your aids.

When you come back to the canter, expect the three beat but be prepared to stick to a not-canter even at this stage.

What happened to me might happen to you as well - the more patient you can be, the sooner the canter will come on its own. To your delight, you might find that the horse offers the three-beat soon after he releases his topline.

26 The Dreaded Rein-Lame: A Mystery

* Note: This chapter is intended to help find solutions for a rider-induced problem, not to mask underlying health issues. Always see a vet when in doubt.

You know the scene: it is virtually impossible for you to figure out what is wrong. The horse has a mild gimp in his movement, but you cannot pinpoint where it is. He does not appear to be lame, but he isn't sound either.

Your friends watch you ride and they can see it - there is that mild head bobble, the lack of stride in the hind end. But no one agrees on one verdict. One friend says it is the left hind leg, another thinks it is the front right. While you ride, you think it is somewhere front and back but it really is hard to tell.

You go through all the tried and true solutions. You even bring the vet out, and on that particular day, she sees nothing. On the lunge line, your horse presents even striding and no head bob.

But you know it's there.

Or maybe, your vet does see something. After extensive (and expensive) radiographs, there is nothing to be found. There is no swelling, no irritation, no injury. You give your horse some time off (while he runs around the pasture in circles at a gallop, showing no sign of discomfort) but as soon as you start your regular riding routine again, the mystery lameness resurfaces.

Does this scenario have a familiar ring to it?

If so, you are not alone.

******

Mystery lamenesses come in all shapes and sizes, but the most common characteristic they share is that they are hard to identify, diagnose and pinpoint. They may come and go, or they may linger for weeks on end. The key is that the "lameness" is mild and generally unidentifiable.

First we must check every other possibility to ensure that all the bases are covered.

Then, it is time to consider the one thing we often fail to recognize as a possible source of discomfort for the horse: our own riding technique. It stands to reason that horses will reflect any stressors that are put on their bodies - and riding can be one factor that is demanding enough to become detrimental to the horse over time.

Common Symptoms

Most mystery lamenesses can be blamed on unreleased tension in the horse's body. This might occur during riding, while the rider is mounted. Often, the lameness is not evident when the horse is moving around freely in the paddock.

Some horses tighten behind the saddle in the lumbosacral region, where the lumbar vertebrae stop and the sacrum begins. This area tends to be a weak zone and prolonged tension in the area can translate into uneven steps and lame-like symptoms in either the front end or the hind end. Hip problems can also be connected to the l-s joint.

Always work to reduce tension during the ride. By finding subtle releases, you can help your horse find his "happy place."

When you ride circles, does your horse have a habit of making small circles in one direction and large ones in the other direction? The size difference is likely due to shoulder tension (which goes hand-in-hand with lack of hind end engagement - see below). This type of front-end lameness comes and goes but is usually present in turns and corners (less obvious on straight lines).

The root of this problem is that horses generally travel in a crooked manner. If action is not taken to address the crookedness in their movement, ligaments and tendons in the shoulders may become affected.

Finally, another type of mystery lameness can be due to lack of engagement of the hind end. If a horse is not taught early in his riding career to reach underneath the body with a deep, strong stride, the hind end development may suffer. Without a strong hind end action to support the weight of the horse and rider, you may find the horse falling heavily to the forehand. You might notice heavy sounding footfalls, tripping, inconsistent stride lengths, heavy contact, and a generally unhappy and unwilling attitude. Eventually, the wear and tear on the horse's front legs can lead to ligament and tendon damage that appears in the form of an on-again, off-again lameness.

Most of the time, regardless of how the lameness appears, the horse is not "forward" enough in all the gaits.

What to do?

1. Become very aware of tension during riding.

Some horses truck along calmly, willingly working even with tight muscular tension. It is easy to overlook the tightness of movement because of the horse's generous character. Learn how to spot the tension, or better yet, how to feel it. Identify where the horse is blocking the energy so that you can take steps to address it.

Find a good instructor who can teach you how to help the horse release tension - whether it is mental or physical - as much as possible during every ride. You can imagine that if the horse is moving in tension almost all the time, there will inevitably be painful repercussions in the long run.

Finding techniques to release the topline of the horse and encourage strong, bold movement will help your horse let go of the blocks that are holding him back from completing his strides.

2. Keep your horse moving straight, even on circles and bends.

A horse can move crooked on a straight line or even on a circle. Often, a horse prefers one side to another, putting too much weight on one shoulder and leg.

It is the task of the rider to identify the strong (and tight) side of the horse and develop stretching techniques to encourage even development of the horse's muscling.

3. Help your horse find his "happy place" as often as possible through the ride.

As mentioned earlier, it is possible for a rider to teach her horse to enjoy being ridden. The better you know your horse, the more you will be able to "play" while you work.

Horses that enjoy their rides are generally more willing, giving and supple in their movements.

4. Start with and end the ride with a balanced, rhythmical stretchy trot, canter and finally walk.

There is no replacement to the stretchy walk, trot and canter. It is a great way to loosen the horse during the warm-up, and the best way to wrap up the day's lessons. When the horse lifts his back and reaches down and out with the nose, the top line muscles have an opportunity to stretch and release. Since the neck is attached to the withers, and the withers to the large muscles over the top of the back, the stretch can reach far back toward the hips.

Once horses know how to stretch, they look forward to the release and often announce their pleasure through snorts and licking and chewing. The stretch is a way to consolidate all that was done during the ride and is an excellent way to come to a calm and relaxing end.

*****

There are likely many more ways to teach a horse suppleness and release of the muscles. The key point is to become aware of the tension and learn how to address it. As you improve your riding skill, and learn more techniques (and "tools") to draw from, you will be able to pinpoint the cause of the lameness and then the solution.

Next, we will discuss specific suggestions on what to do to resolve rein lameness while riding.

27 Stepping Out of Rein Lameness

Some people call it "rein lame".

Other people blame everything under the sun.

But we know that it is often caused by incorrect riding.

You know what I'm talking about - it is the kind of riding that allows the horse to move crookedly. It's about the riding that does not acknowledge (recognize?) that the horse is constantly traveling on the forehand, pounding the front legs into the sand day after day with no improvement.

It ends up being demonstrated by the horse with a shuffling or running gait, the pinned ears, the tense body - even though his legs move and the "buttons" work (sometimes), even the non-horsey onlooker can pick up on the horse's misery.

Most of all, the problems are obvious in the horse's movement. A judge might call it "losing rhythm" or "uneven." A coach might notice that the horse limps when on circles or turns.

Although it is easy to overlook the inconsistencies, a careful observer might be able to see bad steps. On the horse's back, you feel the horse taking limping steps, although it is difficult to identify which leg or where the limping comes from. The vet sees the tightness and tension but further diagnosis identifies nothing wrong at all.

Often, problems caused by riding can be fixed with riding. It is just a matter of having strategies to counteract the problems.

What to do?

1. Step out (weight to the outside shoulder). This "step" can be one step or several steps. For a younger or less experienced horse, you can actually allow the horse to drift out into an almost leg-yield. The step out can be done both on a circle or on a straight line.

Regardless of where the horse is positioned, the step must be initiated by the inside hind leg. Use your inside seat and leg to initiate the step to the outside.

2. Create a bend. Stiffness and crookedness are the main reasons for allowing a build-up of tension. The inside seat and leg also help to develop a bend in the horse's body. However, you can regulate the amount of bend - it can be fairly shallow especially for the stiffest horse. You can work your way up to a deeper bend as the tension falls away.

3. Use the outside leg behind the girth to capture the horse's hip and to prevent him from swinging it out. There always has to be an outside leg to create a "wall" to help the horse know just how far to step out.

Keep the horse's body straight but do a mild leg-yield into the corner. The inside hind leg reaches further underneath the body.

4. Use the outside rein to prevent the neck from swinging to the inside. Of course you must use the outside rein! A floppy outside rein will encourage the crookedness that is probably already plaguing your horse. If there is nothing to provide an outside "wall" for the bend, there will be no bend! Let the horse curve into the outside rein. That outside rein is also going to govern just how far you want the horse to step out (#1).

5. Use the inside rein to maintain flexion to prevent stiffness all the way from the jaw to the tail. The inside rein has only one job: to maintain a soft flexion. Keep the horse looking to the inside of the bend (circle) by using a light (on/off) contact.

Do not let the nose point to the outside, but also avoid pulling the horse into the bend or circle with just the inside rein. There should always be mini-releases when the inside rein is being applied, or you will block the ability of the inside hind leg from having a chance to reach under the body.

6. Finish with impulsion. Once the horse has stepped out and because of the movement, loosened up and released some tension, ask for a bit more of a step underneath from the hind legs. Remember to always finish any lateral work with an increase in stride length and energy.

How often you use the "step out" depends on how stiff the horse is and how often the bad steps occur.

The key is to catch the bad steps early, and then work with the bend and shift of weight to the outside to get the horse to release his tightness and tension.

The Results

If you notice a wider lateral step through the shoulder (to the outside), and less of a limping feeling, then you know you are on the right track.

If the horse becomes calmer/stronger/bouncier/rounder, you know this is the way to go. If the horse gives you a snort, a chew on the bit, and soft ears, you know you've hit the jackpot!

Essentially, you are looking for the release of tension that allows the horse to use his muscles to bear weight and produce the locomotion. You are seeking a condition that allows the horse to NOT put excess strain on the joints, tendons, ligaments and skeleton.

Ideally, you are doing your best to put the horse into his happy place, so he can enjoy his work and develop in a positive manner.

There are likely many other exercises that can address the same problem.

P.S. Can you achieve the same results with a step (or steps) to the inside? YES! All the same ideas apply - then, you can "play" to the inside AND the outside of the circle/bend on a straight line and develop both sides of the horse's body!

Section 5: The Results

28 Twenty Ways Horse Riding Becomes Life Itself

At first, horse riding is just like any other skill you want to learn. You put some effort in and eventually become more effective as time goes on.

At some point, things begin to change. Somehow, without you necessarily knowing about it, the lessons the horses have taught you start materializing in your daily activities, even when the circumstances have nothing at all to do with horses.

So you could say that horses are our teachers. Not only do we grow in terms of physical ability, but perhaps even more so, we grow in character.

While we develop as riders, we also grow as human beings. Situations that used to affect us one way no longer bother us in the same manner, not because the circumstances themselves are any different, but more due to how we have learned to deal with them.

Then we realize that the true teachers are the horses themselves. All we have to do is learn to listen.

Horses and riding parallel life itself.

Horse riding becomes life when...

1. The patience you develop working with your horse becomes the patience you use with your friends and colleagues.

2. The body language you learn to communicate with becomes your source of confidence during group activities.

3. The coordination you learn on the back of the horse keeps you safe from unexpected physical mishaps.

4. Heavy lifting/pulling/pushing/hoof cleaning develops your strength enough to allow you to fluidly function under heavy loads when needed.

5. Facing your fears while on another's four legs teaches you how to have courage in the face of life's many difficulties.

6. You learn to temper your (often over-scheduled) daily routines by slowing down to meet the simplicity of horse life.

7. The leadership skills your horse teaches you carries into your work and relationship interactions.

8. The self-confidence you develop from knowing you can influence a powerful animal seeps into every interaction you have with people.

9. You learn from horses that it's okay for things to get worse, because after things get worse, they always get better.

10. You discover that taking shortcuts might not be to your benefit in the long run; some things have to take the time they need to take.

11. When certain maneuvers get a little difficult (like riding through a corner), all you need is a little extra impulsion to smooth things out.

12. Sometimes, you just have to let go (especially when the horse bucks and bucks)!

13. In general, riding (life) isn't about brute strength - it's about gentle technique and strategy.

14. There is no such thing as a day off - you begin to value the rewards that hard work reaps.

15. The work has to get done whether you feel up to it or not - so it becomes easier to fulfill responsibilities because you know *how* to get the work done.

16. You understand completely how asking nicely is always better than demanding.

17. There is no such thing as instant gratification. There is only hard work and step-by-step development.

18. Perfection is always aspired to, but rarely reached!

19. The path is more important than the end result.

20. Although we all have our own "conformation faults" that might work against us, we can overcome almost anything with some time and effort.

29 Ten Tips For the Average Rider

Are you an average rider? You know the type - the one who has to work hard for one step forward and two steps back.

Are you the one who has to spend hours and hours finding your seat, or coordinating your hands and legs to *finally* not interfere with your horse?

Then join the club!

We are the ones who drool wistfully at those riders that seem to just get on the horse and blend into the movement with nary a thought. We are the ones who need lessons broken down into small, achievable steps that eventually develop into just one coordinated movement. We practice, practice and then practice some more, even while seeming to make only minimal progress.

If you resemble the above scenarios, don't despair. Enjoy the following tips to get through those average rider moments that we all experience from time to time.

1. Find a good teacher.

I use the word "teacher" because the skill development required at the basic levels requires someone that can impart knowledge as well as technique. A good instructor can explain the physiology of movement. The best instructors can direct you to find "feels" for yourself. Detailed explanations and clarity of purpose can make the learning curve much easier and even quicker for us average riders.

2. Be patient.

Cut yourself some slack. Then cut your horse some slack. Always seek correct posture, aids, and movements but do it with a sense of humility and gratefulness. Never forget that your horse is working for you and choosing to humor your requests! If something goes wrong, problem solve and patiently redirect your horse's behavior.

3. Practice.

As much as we would like short-cuts, secret methods or fancy expensive gimmicks that will open the world of riding to us, there is no other way to truly become an effective, compassionate rider than to practice. And so we must.

4. Accept your limitations.

Some of us not-as-young riders discover that no matter how hard we try, some parts of our bodies simply never seem to respond the way we would hope!

For example, ligaments and tendons become shortened over time and less resilient. Lower legs have more trouble staying still, or releasing our lower backs to follow the horse becomes more of a challenge. We need to acknowledge that developing more flexible bodies will take longer and harder work. We might need to seek other avenues of physical development such as yoga or Pilates to find that release we are looking for.

5. Find your comfortable un-comfort.

Despite knowing our challenges, we need to constantly seek improvement. Beware of becoming the rider who never develops their skills year after year. Always push yourself past your comfort zone and know that confusion and frustration are part of the learning process. Difficult rides are a good sign that you are going to make a breakthrough (sooner or later)!

6. Enjoy the moment.

Even if we struggle, and certainly through our grandest rides, we must enjoy the moments we get to share with our equine friends. For it is the moment that is what we are here for.

7. Persevere.

Sometimes, it might feel like you are never going to make that breakthrough that you've been looking for. The key at this juncture is to be so determined and stubborn that you will be willing to come back and try again tomorrow and the next day and the day after that.

8. Set goals.

Set long term goals, then develop realistically achievable short-term goals. Be flexible but have an intended path. Even if you don't meet your goals, they will serve to direct your efforts and give you perspective.

9. Read, watch, imitate.

Look out for inspiration. Read the books of the masters as well as contemporary riders. In this day and age of the Internet, having access to excellent video footage of lessons, clinic rides, and show footage is at your fingertips.

Watch many riders, define what you like in a good ride and study. Then, go and try it yourself. Imitation is the first step to learning a skill set. Watch and try. Get feedback from your instructor. Once you have developed a skill, you can easily make the skill "yours" by adding something new or specific to your horse's needs.

10. Keep practicing.

Develop a routine. Follow a system. But keep at it. There is no other way.

30 Five Life Lessons From Horses

If we can learn anything from horses, it is that many concepts hold true as clearly in life as they do in the world of horses. If you listen carefully, you can find answers to your questions from every interaction with the horses.

These little tidbits can help you along your path, reminding you of important insights that can serve to guide you as you live life and develop, learn and grow. Here are just five:

5. Keep Finding Your "Edge"

In riding, you are always evaluating where you are with your horse. You try to ask your horse to bend a little deeper, step a little stronger, swing a little bouncier. You work on aiding a little softer, sitting a little deeper, developing a more consistent contact. Whenever you have achieved a level of mastery in a skill, you assess where you're at and look for the next step. Riding is an act of constant learning, improving and discovery.

The concept of finding your "edge" is about knowing where you are at the moment, and pushing yourself that one bit further toward either a new level of understanding/ability, or toward an entirely new skill. Day-to-day life can be that way too.

Socrates was the first to identify the paradox of learning: the more you know, the more you realize you know nothing.

There are so many levels of understanding in any one thing. Just as you can learn a riding skill deeper-stronger-looser or better, you can similarly develop your skills and understanding in all aspects of life.

So get out there, learn, do, and keep on finding your edge! Becoming a lifelong learner is not just a nice-sounding cliché - it is a way of life!

4. It's All About Finding the Right Balance

Gravity sucks the same way for everyone!

Learning to find a useful, correct balance in horseback riding takes time and perseverance. However, once you have achieved even a basic level of balance, things flow more smoothly, riding becomes easier, and your horse becomes happier!

Similarly, when you can find balance in your life - the balance between work, play, studying, and doing something for your self, things somehow seem to go smoother, easier, and you might even find yourself becoming happier!

3. Find Your Happy Place!

Help a horse find his happy place, and he will be enthusiastic, cooperative and confident in his work. He will be loose, forward-thinking and perky-eared.

2. Never Get Bored

From the outside, it looks like the horse and rider are going round and round and round in circles. From the inside, you are so focused on the process of developing so many things WHILE you go around those circles that you never have a chance to get bored! The same goes for the horse - keep the training varied and comfortable, and the horse will rarely sour from the work. Anything that feels good, whether on circles or on a trail, can be enjoyable for the horse and keep him mentally coming back for more.

Riding horses opens up a world of personal growth and learning.

Finding the things you love to do in life will leave you satisfied and content. Finding a sense of purpose and reaching for that ultimate goal will make a mystery out of the mundane, keeping things fresh and challenging for years to come.

1. Learn to Listen

Anyone who has spent time with horses could agree that listening is key - no, CRITICAL - to experiencing the best our equines have to give. Regardless of whether you are riding or on the ground, there is a constant communication occurring between you and your horse.

Even if you don't know it, or can't interpret the communication, it is happening and your horse is picking up signals from your (in)actions. As you develop your horse "speak", you will realize how much you can read from your horse's behavior and subtle communications.

The same goes with life. If you can listen carefully enough, you can "hear" so many critical messages that are sent your way daily! More importantly, the concept of listening to our fellow humans, from a personal level to a global level, is critical to the development of humankind. Communication is key in all aspects - from making friends as children, to learning skills at school, to maintaining personal relationships, to holding jobs and securing business deals - life is communication. And the most critical step is listening.

31 17 Wise Reflections - From the Horse's Mouth!

My horse, Annahi, is full of words of wisdom for those horses around her who are willing to listen.

She has quite the resume and has been there, done it all: she did lessons, participated (and won her share of awards) in western performance and dressage shows, rode in parades and even became a reliable enough trail horse to lead many a public ride. She has learned much through her many and varied experiences, and now, at the ripe old age of 25 (her birthday was in June), she decided she'd like to share her wisdom by writing a short post on my blog.

Although her intention is to help improve the daily trials of fellow equines, I'm sure us humans can benefit too. So here are her words of wisdom.

1. Stop and smell the roses - err... chomp on a bit of grass (especially when things seem to be getting a little hectic during the ride)!

There's always a good time to stop for a leisurely munch, but one of the best times is while your rider is desperately kicking to get you moving! Take extra time and go for that one last mouthful before you bring your head up. Then, dive down for one more bite!

Annahi

2. If your feet get stuck in mud, give a good buck and carry on!

For some of us Princesses, there's nothing worse than the extract-your-shoe sucking action of deep mud. What do to? Just swish your tail and throw in a good buck! Oh, and yes, make sure that your human can hold on.

3. There's nothing better than mutual grooming.

You scratch my back and I'll scratch yours - we horses

invented this!

4. If there isn't enough grass to eat, head for the trees.

Leaves make good alternative nutritional sources - so even if there still is some grass in the field - give leaves a try!

5. When you're hot, find a full water trough and splash around!

Ahhh... there's nothing quite like a splash in the water trough on a hot day! Make sure it was just scrubbed and filled before you start digging your muddy hooves into it. Flail away and get as much water out as possible! Humans enjoy filling water troughs.

6. Put your ears forward and charm the one with the treats.

Put on that cuddly, bright-eyed, ears perked face and no human will be able to deny you those delectable yummies! If you know how to make that look, you'll always get what you want!

7. Releasing your topline makes it easier to carry the load.

There is no better way to travel! Let go of your tension and put a little bounce into your step. All you have to do is let go, let loose and swing! The rest just flows along easily!

8. Snooze short but often.

Sleep often. Sleep well. Eat in between!

9. Clear out the flies from your face with a reliable swish buddy.

Sometimes, a friend is all you need to help you solve your problems. Find a swish buddy and there will be no more flies on your face! Just be ready to give back.

10. Jump high enough to make it over the fence.

Well, if there are any obstacles in your way, you just have to figure out how to jump high enough! A little practice and that should do the trick.

11. Give a loud, wet snort to acknowledge your approval.

Deep snorts mean so much. They mean that you're happy, breathing well, even soft in your muscles. Be sure to let your human feel the depth of your contentment and snort ON them when they are standing in front of you!

12. Slow the legs to float longer.

It is possible to go too fast at any gait. Have you ever found yourself scrambling to get your footing? Make it easier on yourself and slow down to bounce higher and stride longer. Then you will feel this floating sensation that just can't be beat!

13. Go balanced into the corner, and full steam ahead coming out!

Collect a bit before the corner, but be sure to add a little "oomph" on the way out. That little extra energy can set you up smoothly for the rest of the ride.

14. Bending left and right makes for a better straight ahead.

They say that going straight needs a good left AND right side. So get out there and be your ambidextrous best!

15. Always have someone on the lookout.

When you feel a nap coming on, be sure that one of your trusty herd members is prepared to stand watch over you.

16. Life is all about finding the right rhythm.

That's what they say, and it's the truth. There is nothing better than a steady, reliable rhythm - whether in walk, trot, canter or in everyday life. So get out there and find your rhythm - and enjoy!

17. Always give before you take.

This one goes without saying. Take the half-halt, for instance. The best half-halt is the one that gives first, then holds for rebalance, then gives again. And so it should be in life.

32 Top Ten Reasons to Ride A Horse

What are the reasons you ride horses? There must be as many reasons to ride horses are there are people who ride. For those of us that are bitten with "the bug" that is horses, there are few reasons *not* to get on a horse's back!

10. The chance to be in the great outdoors.

Spring, summer, winter or fall - you can find things to do with horses. As you participate in your various activities, you become so much more a part of the outdoor environment. Although conditions might not always be the best, you learn to work with the weather and appreciate Mother Nature's artwork. You also learn to take better care of yourself as well as your horses in response to the weather conditions of the season.

9. The joy of being in the world of horses.

You learn new communication skills when you interact with horses. By their very nature, horses are not the same as the pets we are familiar with. They are large, they are prey animals and they allow us to ride them!

8. The privilege of being allowed to sit on the back of such a magnificent animal and seeing the world from his perspective.

Life on four legs, several hands high is certainly different than what we are used to! Not only does the act of riding bring us new and (at first) unfamiliar experiences, but the places you can literally go is good enough reason to ride.

Thanks to horses and riding, I have traveled all over my own province, in other provinces, and in other countries. Certainly without horses as a reason to pursue these activities, our lives would be lacking.

7. Exercise that is so similar to our own movement that it is healing for ourselves.

Riding horses gives our body the movement it relishes and needs. In the case of hippotherapy, riding can literally be therapeutic. Also, riding as a sport benefits the body and mind in many ways.

6. The variety of activities and events you can participate in if you ride a horse.

Once you get involved in the horse world, you will be amazed at all the activities and events that you might participate in! From weekly riding lessons to trail riding to vaulting to fundraising rides - the sky is the limit! There are simply too many events to list here. The clincher is that those who don't participate in riding do not have the opportunity to even begin to understand such vibrant experiences.

**Horses can take you to some of the most
beautiful places on Earth.**

5. Learning skills that promote coordination, timing, rhythm, balance, core strength and much more.

Skills, skills and skills!

Skill development is one large component of what horseback riding is all about. As you grow as a rider, you'll be amazed at how your physical abilities progress. You will be sure to improve in all the above areas as well as in your mental skills such as problem-solving and determination.

4. The self-development process that goes hand-in-hand with skill development.

Self-confidence, self-control, patience, empathy - all these and more traits will be developed as you progress through your riding experiences. There is no way around it. If you ride, you will grow as a human being.

3. The life-long, ever changing learning process that is horses and riding.

If you like learning, and feel a pang of excitement when you discover something new, horse riding is for you! The catch is that you would do well to enjoy this feeling of discomfort-before-learning-something-new because it will happen again and again - even years into your riding career!

2. Learning to problem solve effectively and ride with enough tact to improve the health and well-being of the horse.

There is nothing more motivating than to realize that one day, you will ride well enough to be able to give back to the horses you ride. As your skills develop, your aids will support, redirect, enhance and even improve the horse's natural tendencies.

One day, you might notice that your horse is physically healthier and mentally happier because of the riding experiences he receives - from little ol' you!

1. The ultimate release, and the feeling of oneness when everything is going right.

Well, though rarely realized, this togetherness is what will keep you coming back for more. Once you feel the connection, you will be able to persevere through every negative experience, setback and obstacle. Because once you have achieved harmony, you will know why you ride.

33 Twenty Signs That Your Horse Benefits From Your Riding

Do you sometimes wonder if what you are doing with the horse is beneficial to him? Are you occasionally unsure of how well your riding/training program is going?

One of the surest ways to know if you are being helpful to your horse (with your riding) is to listen to your horse. If you know how to interpret his signs and communications, all your questions will essentially be answered, especially in terms of how well your riding is going.

Are you following your horse's movement?

Are you asking for/allowing enough impulsion?

Do you "commit" your body to the forward motion you're asking for?

Is the horse learning to/allowed to stretch over the topline so he can more effectively use his musculature to carry you?

These questions (and more) can be answered by correctly reading the horse's responses to your requests. Although many of these signs can be seen from the ground or during groundwork, the advantage of these horsey "yes answers" is that they can be identified *while you ride*. Here are some ways to know if you are on the right track:

- the horse gives an emphatic snort.

- the horse licks and chews through the movement.

- the horse is calmer at the end of the ride than he was at the beginning.

- the horse's topline looks fuller, even just moments after the ride.

- the horse's stride becomes longer, bouncier and more cadenced.

- the horse bends deeper with less rein aid.

- movements come easier after a few repetitions.

- the horse reaches higher/wider/longer with the hind end.

- the eyes get soft.

- the horse's expression is calm.

- the horse's ears fall (or sometimes flop) gently to the side unless he is "listening" to your aids, at which point the ear will momentarily come back to you.

- the horse softens his poll/jaw upon contact.

- transitions come easily.

- bends and turns are softly negotiated.

- he can stay straighter in his body while moving on or off the rail.
- the horse engages his hind end quickly and easily without tensing or bracing through the additional energy.

- the back becomes softer, especially in the trot.

- the tail lifts slightly during movement.

- the hind legs track up or overttrack.

- the horse's overall body outline rounds rather than hollows.

After-the-ride happy expression.

A Final Word

I wasn't one of those riders who hopped into the saddle for the first time and rode off into the sunset like I'd been riding my whole life. I didn't grow up in a horsey family or within the horsey set.

I never even met my first real-life horse until I was over 10 years of age. As it happened, my introduction to real horses came in a roundabout way. One day while we were on holiday, my father decided to treat me to a (he thought) one-time trail riding treat. I remember the day well. He actually rode with me, as I was too young to go on my own – he had his horse and I had mine.

I knew the moment I saw the horse that this was what I had been waiting for my whole life. After that very special ride, my parents could no longer keep my horse passion at bay. Having never been around horses and living the good suburban life meant that there was little access to anything horsey other than books.

So with much pleading and pleasing, I managed to talk them into riding lessons at a facility too far away to go more than once a week. That brief beginning led to what I knew I must do: include horses in my life.

But despite my natural athleticism in all things sport, riding became one of the biggest physical challenges of my life. I suspect it has something to do with the 1000-pound partner that could easily weigh in to the conversation with his own opinions.

Through many and varied experiences, I learned to physically coordinate many parts of the body that I didn't even know existed! I devised training schedules, fun riding excursions, overnight barn stays and eventually, stepped into the show ring.

I made friends I would have never met otherwise, revealed a love for nature and all things outdoors and over the years, made the most important discovery of all: I learned about my *self*.

Although your journey might not be the same as mine, this one truth will likely follow you as it did me. You'd better be prepared to discover and accept your weaknesses as well as strengths, for these great creatures serve as honest and reliable mirrors of our own efforts. They also invite us into a world that seems so unlike ours yet filled with parallels that can inform us in our daily lives.

If you learn how to listen to the horses, and how to recognize their body language, you can become adequate interpreters of these amazing animals. It's not some secret otherworldly skill. Just be quiet and sensitive enough, learn the body language signs, and the world of horses will open up to you in a most organic manner.

Riding through listening can guide you on your path to becoming a more effective rider - for your pleasure and safety, and for your horse's as well.

If you enjoyed this book, go to

www.HorseListening.com

for new articles about horses, riding

and life in general!

Keep an eye out for the second book

from the Horse Listening collection!

ABOUT THE AUTHOR

Kathy Farrokhzad is an Equine Canada certified instructor with more than 20 years of teaching and training experience in several riding disciplines. Her "real job" experience as a professional school teacher enables her to use teaching strategies that present information in a step-by-step, clear manner that clarifies and instructs.

A writer from a very young age, Kathy has had articles published in national equine magazines. She has a monthly column in The Rider and regularly contributes to equestrian association newsletters.

Owned by four horses, Kathy spends much of her spare time in and around the barn. She has enjoyed learning something new and different from each horse. They are the "models" of the pictures used in her articles as well as in this book.

She is also the writer of the blog, HorseListening.com.

CPSIA information can be obtained at www.ICGtesting.com
Printed in the USA
LVOW04s0106100215

426388LV00027B/648/P

9 780993 669606